ONE ANOTHER

Other Books by Thomas A. Jones

No One Like Him: Jesus and His Message

Strong in the Grace: Reclaiming the Heart of the Gospel

God's Perfect Plan for Imperfect People: The Message of Ephesians

Letters to New Disciples: Practical Advice for Those Who Have Decided to Follow Jesus

The Prideful Soul's Guide to Humility (co-authored with Michael Fontenot)

To Live Is Christ (co-authored with Sheila Jones)

Mind Change: A Biblical Path to Overcoming Life's Challenges

In Search of a City: An Autobiographical Perspective on a Remarkable but Controversial Movement

The Kingdom of God, Volume 1 (with Steve D. Brown)

The Kingdom of God, Volume 2 (with Steve D. Brown)

The Kingdom of God, Volume 3

All are available at

ONE ANOTHER

*Transformational Relationships
in the Body of Christ*

THOMAS JONES & STEVE BROWN

One Another
©2019 by Illumination Publishers
6010 Pinecreek Ridge Court, Spring Texas 77379
www.ipibooks.com

All rights reserved.
No part of this book may be duplicated, copied, translated,
reproduced or stored mechanically or electronically
without specific, written permission of
Good Book Press.

All Scripture quotations, unless indicated, are taken from
the NEW INTERNATIONAL VERSION.
Copyright ©1973, 1978, 1984 by the International Bible Society.
Used by permission of Zondervan Publishing House.
All rights reserved.

The "NIV" and "New International Version" trademarks
are registered in the United States Patent Trademark Office
by the International Bible Society.
Use of either trademarks requires the permission of
the International Bible Society.

Scripture quotations marked HCSB are taken from the
Holman Christian Standard Bible®, Copyright © 1999, 2000, 2002, 2003 by
Holman Bible Publishers. Used by permission. Holman Christian Standard
Bible®, Holman CSB®, and HCSB® are federally registered trademarks of
Holman Bible Publishers.

Printed in the United States of America
ISBN 978-1-948450-84-3

Cover Design: Jennifer Maugel
Interior Design: Thais Gloor

To the Greater Nashville Church
and those in the Andean family of
churches in South America.
We see you striving to
live out these truths.

Contents

Introduction 8

Chapter 1: Relationships at the Center of the Target 13

Chapter 2: Relationships According to God's Grace 25

Chapter 3: Loving One Another 33

Chapter 4: Accepting One Another 39

Chapter 5: Belonging to One Another 47

Chapter 6: Teaching and Admonishing One Another 55

Chapter 7: Confessing Sins to One Another 65

Chapter 8: Bearing One Another's Burdens 77

Chapter 9: Encouraging One Another 87

Chapter 10: Spurring One Another On 97

Chapter 11: Reconciling with One Another 107

Chapter 12: Forgiving One Another 119

Chapter 13: "One Another" in Groups 127

Chapter 14: The Logical Conclusion: Let Us Begin 137

Appendix 1: Philippians: A Study of Relationships 151

Appendix 2: Discipling Relationships and the Holy Spirit 159

Introduction

The New Testament is a radical book. Its central character had nothing to do with religion as usual. He made scandalous claims, called for sweeping changes, and created a disturbance almost every where he went. But the radical nature of his message is not found in calls for protests or in advocating the value of violence. To the contrary, it is found in his call to welcome the kingdom of God that is breaking into this present age with a call to take love for God and love and responsibility for one another, along with the idea of community, to a dramatically new depth. It is also found in speaking prophetically against religion that is self-focused, autonomous and narcissistic.

To enter the kingdom and become a disciple of Jesus in NT terms was always to become part of the church of God, the *ekklesia* in Greek. The word refers to the community of people who are called together to live together for a special purpose. Unfortunately the English word "church" (which comes from Latin words that refer to the house of a master or lord) does not really communicate to most people the idea of community or fellowship. Accordingly, in many people's minds they can belong to a church and still live life as separately or independently as they please. This was never God's plan.

Call to Involvement

From the very earliest days of the church's existence following the outpouring of the Spirit on Pentecost (Acts 2), it is clear that this was going to mean being involved in one another's lives in the deepest and most far-reaching ways. As we read NT letters to these communities we increasingly see that this involvement was not just to meet our need to socialize or have friends, but *it was to be transformational in nature.* The way these relationships were conducted was to be used by the Spirit of God to bring about changes in people's lives so that through this connection and dynamic with one another, they would grow and develop and mature into the likeness of Jesus, no less.

"Be transformed," Paul writes, "through the renewing of your minds" (Romans 12:2), but the verses that follow in that same chapter make it clear that such transformation was not something that would occur as one solely meditated on God and his truth in isolation. It would come where his people lived out God's message in relationships and community as those who belonged to one another (v5) and as those devoted to one another (v10).

Dynamic Relationships

"One another" (one word, *allelon,* in Greek) is a phrase that occurs thirty-seven times in the NT letters in the New International Version (NIV) and is used almost exclusively in these letters to refer to the things that should, and in a few cases should not, characterize relationships among believers. When looked at together, and in context, these passages give us a comprehensive picture of dynamic relationships in which disciples of Jesus are accepted, loved, encouraged, challenged, helped and built up. They show us that the body of Christ is a place where there is to be confession, forgiveness and an eagerness to bear one another's burdens. A close look at these texts makes it clear that God sees these relationships as crucial to the fulfilling of his purposes and the fulfilling of our destiny. There is nothing peripheral or secondary about the concept of "one another."

Beyond this, numerous other principles are given to us for building and enhancing relationships even though the phrase "one another" may not be used. Arguably, Paul's letter to the Philippians was entirely about relationships (see appendix 1), though in that letter he uses *allelon* only once.

Our goal in this book is to show that walking with one another is central to our walk with God and means being involved in meaningful give and take in one another's lives.

Not a Common Understanding

As we begin this study, it is important to recognize that we are swimming against the tide of religious tradition and sometimes even well-known highly respected religious teachers. We were struck recently to see that such esteemed thinkers as Augustine, Aquinas and even John Calvin saw some kind of dichotomy between our relationship with God and our relationship with one another. They saw the former being far more important than the latter, so much so that each believed that fellowship with one another would play a minor role, if even that, in eternal life. Calvin somewhat stunningly put it this way: "To be in Paradise and live with God is not to speak to each other and be heard by each other, but is only to enjoy God, to feel his good will and to rest in him."[1]

Combine some of this classical teaching with Western individualism and you get a view of Christian practice that is far from the New Testament's view. Did you ever see an old movie where deep sea divers were dropped into the depths in heavy suits with big round helmets? Each diver was given air through a tube that entered his helmet and was connected to the air supply at the surface.

Many years ago I heard someone say that when you see

---

1. John Calvin, *Corpus Reformatorum* 33.227.

Christians taking the Lord's Supper today it is much like this deep sea scenario. It is as though each person is in his or her own isolated chamber with a line going up to God. In contrast to NT teaching (1 Corinthians 11:17-34), there is little sense of connection to one another. This comment made about the Lord's Supper could be made about many people's Christian experience in general.

I have had many conversations with people who seldom miss a church service or a mass, but when asked who they are involved with in a deep way in that assembly, they usually admit there is no one. Even if they have some relationships, they are often far from what we will see in the passages we will examine.

Like everything else about following Jesus, these crucial relationships will not happen without repentance. We must recognize that we are desperately in need of a major mind change, and we must be prepared to receive the kingdom as a little child, allowing Jesus to lead us some places we never thought we would go (and maybe are even fearful of going).

While these relationships will certainly cost us something—and sometimes a great deal, we pray you will see this book as an invitation to a richer life and to an opportunity to show the world the glory of God in a special way.

Our Friendship

The two of us first became acquainted with one another after Steve was diagnosed with multiple sclerosis in 1994. Steve was aware that Tom had been living with MS for some time, and the two of us began to communicate by phone, with Tom in Boston and Steve in Dallas. Our first actual meeting was on African soil when we both attended a leadership conference in Johannesburg, South Africa. Though we continued to stay in touch, ironically, we would not see each other again until we were both attending a meeting in Jerusalem in 1997.

As God would have it, the Browns moved to Nashville, Tennessee, in 2002, and the Joneses also moved to that same area in 2005. Our relationship continued to grow, and this book grew out of a series of classes on this topic that we taught in the summer of 2007 in the Greater Nashville Church.

As we jump into this necessary and exciting subject, we want to be clear: we make no claim to being some kind of "relationship gurus" or even to being especially good at relationships. We are writing out of a conviction that this is the real stuff of discipleship and life in the kingdom of God. We are committed to growing and learning about how to improve the depth and quality of our relationships till the kingdom comes in all its finality and fullness.

Making It Real

We want this book to be as practical as possible. At the end of each chapter we will include questions for you or, even better, for your group to discuss. To get started, take a minute to think about the following:

1. Write down the name of the person with whom you have your best relationship in this church.
2. On a scale from one to ten, with ten being the very best, how would you rate your relationship in terms of openness and spiritual depth?
3. On a scale from one to ten, how do you think they would rate your commitment to the relationship?
4. Write down the name of someone with whom you know it would be good for you and for them to have a better relationship.

Relationships at the Center of the Target

More than thirty years ago I (Tom) was introduced to an idea that profoundly affected the way I look at Scripture. Wendell Broom, a professor of missions at a Christian university, pointed out that many people look at the will of God as revealed in Scripture and see it like a set of dominoes where everything in God's will is the same size and the same weight. (Ignore the numbers on the blocks and just see the dimensions of the blocks themselves in Figure 1.)

Figure 1

So in their minds, to give one example, the issue of a deacon's qualifications or what type of music to use in worship would be the same weight as something like justice and mercy. The reasoning is that anything related to God is just as important as anything else related to God. Not unexpectedly, such an approach often leads to endless controversies over smaller details.

However, Broom pointed out that when Jesus looked at God's will, he did not see it like a set of dominoes as much as he saw it like a target (Figure 2). With Jesus, certain things were dead center

Figure 2

or more central than others. Other issues were still within Scripture and within the will of God, but were more peripheral rings.

Where did the professor get this idea? From Matthew 23 where Jesus says,

> "Woe to you, teachers of the law and Pharisees, you hypocrites! You give a tenth of your spices—mint, dill and cummin. But you have neglected the more important matters of the law—justice, mercy and faithfulness. You should have practiced the latter, without neglecting the former. You blind guides! You strain out a gnat but swallow a camel." (Matthew 23:23-24)

The tithe the Pharisees focused on was found in Scripture, but it clearly was not among what Jesus calls "the more important matters." By neglecting "the weightier matters" (KJV)—the center of the target—and focusing on lesser matters that were easier to keep track of and handle legalistically, they ended up with a great distortion of what God had planned for his people.

While Scripture does not spell out for us what is in the second ring and the third ring, it does make very clear in various ways what things are in the center of the target. Jesus goes on to teach that we should not neglect any of God's will (v23), but he is clear that any practice that omits "the more important matters"—the center of the target—can never bring honor to God.

CENTRALITY OF RELATIONSHIPS

In this book we are affirming that relationships in the body of Christ—and particularly the nature of those relationships—are not in some peripheral area. They are to be found at the center of the target, at the heart of what the kingdom is all about. If we have any interest in being faithful to God and in being a serious disciple of Jesus Christ in this world, the nature of our relationships with other Christians must be of primary concern. As the kingdom breaks into our present age and God's will is done on earth as it is in heaven, there will be a remarkable difference in kingdom relationships, and seeing to this must be a passion of disciples.

Understanding that this conclusion is not something that should just be assumed, let us look carefully at different places in Scripture where the centrality of relationships is made clear.

1. Matthew 22:37–40

> Jesus replied: "'Love the Lord your God with all your heart and with all your soul and with all your mind.' This is the first and greatest commandment. And the second is like it: 'Love your neighbor as yourself.' All the Law and the Prophets hang on these two commandments."

With Jesus speaking here about the greatest of the commandments, there can be little doubt that we are at the center of the target. Certainly nothing is more in that place than loving God with all one's being. No amount of church activity or even study of Scripture can ever substitute for a personal love for God that permeates every area of life, conversation and practice.

But then Jesus says, "The second is like it." There is a second commandment. It is second, but it is not far behind. It is almost out of his mouth in the same breath. And it is so closely akin to the first, in just how essential and vital it is, that Jesus had to connect the two. What was it? "Love your neighbor as yourself." Jesus makes it clear that relationship with others is intricately tied in with relationship with God.

"All the Law and the Prophets hang on these two commandments," Jesus says. For the Jew he could not have been clearer. For them, the Law and the Prophets encompassed all of God's will, and Jesus is saying, in the words of The Message Bible, "These two commands are pegs; everything in God's Law and the Prophets hangs from them."

But if this passage introduces us to and lays the foundation for the idea that relationships are at the center of God's will, this message will be underscored more specifically in something Jesus said later just to his disciples.

2. John 13:34-35

> "A new command I give you: Love one another. As I have loved you, so you must love one another. By this all men will know that you are my disciples, if you love one another."

How had Jesus loved them? Graciously, unconditionally, sacrificially, honestly (not holding back any truth they needed) and humbly, as their servant (note just a few verses earlier). Now he commands them to love one another just as they have seen and known him to love them. While we are not left to surmise or guess what this means (as many other NT teachings will spell it out for us), if this were the only statement we had to go on, we could develop a rather thorough picture of the kind of relationships Christians ought to have with one another. And if it were the only statement we had, we certainly would have no doubt about how crucial it is for us to develop and practice such an understanding.

This, Jesus says, is the way all men will know we are his disciples. Remarkable! This is so near the center of the target that it will be the distinctive mark by which Christians will be recognized as truly his. We are not in peripheral territory here. Correct doctrine is important, but Jesus does not say, "Men will know you are my disciples by your doctrine." Inspirational assemblies have an important place, but Jesus does not say, "These will convince others that you are mine."

The prophet Isaiah 700 years before Christ looked forward and saw the coming kingdom where disputes would be settled and people would beat their swords (tools of division) into plowshares (tools of peace) (Isaiah 2:4). There would be the seemingly impossible unity of the wolf and the lamb, the leopard and the goat, the calf and the lion—all being led by a little child (Isaiah 11:6–9). Men would protect each other and be for one another a shelter from the wind (Isaiah 32:2). As those in Jesus' church practice his love in their relationships with one another, others will see evidence that the messianic kingdom has come.

Why does Jesus not say something like, "All men will know you are my disciples, when they see your prayer life or your devotion to Scripture"? While we cannot be sure, an educated guess would be that men can pray (Matthew 6:5) and study the Scriptures (Matthew 22:29) for self-serving purposes. But when you see men and women laying down their lives for one another, it looks like Jesus (John 3:16 and 1 John 3:16) and what the Spirit through Isaiah anticipated. Relationships among believers are part of the "more important things" because Jesus clearly put them there.

3. Acts 2:42

> They devoted themselves to the apostles' teaching and to the fellowship, to the breaking of bread and to prayer.

Here we have a description of the first group of believers following the baptism of three thousand on the Day of Pentecost. Luke makes it clear that the apostles, trained by Jesus, were leading these new disciples. As they closely adhered (*proskartereo*—"devoted themselves") to what the apostles taught them, they devoted themselves to "the fellowship, to the breaking of bread and to prayer." Certainly, the second practice followed the first. What they heard from the apostles in all likelihood was what the apostles had heard from Jesus as recorded in John 13:34–35. Their repentance and turning to Jesus was to be lived out in loving others who had also committed themselves to follow him.

But perhaps we see this more specifically when we look closely at this word "fellowship." The word in Greek is *koinonia*. Whereas today the word "fellowship" might bring to mind casual conversation or other lightweight associations, the word *koinonia* referred to much more—to partnership and deep involvement. The word was used outside the New Testament to describe marriage. The New English Bible may best capture the essence of the word with the phrase "sharing together in the common life." *Koinonia* has its root in the word *koinon* which means "common" or "in common." People who experience *koinonia* share a common life—not a casual connection.

This is not the garden club, the poker group or even the Rotary Club we are talking about. This is family, but in another sense, even deeper than normal family. This is the connection of people who are related because they have been baptized into the name of Jesus, born of the Spirit and share the deepest identity, values and goals.

The apostles took seriously what Jesus had taught them and made this commitment to one another a primary teaching for new converts. From day one there was never any question that sharing life together was at the center of the target.

4. Galatians 6:1-2

> Brothers, if someone is caught in a sin, you who are spiritual should restore him gently. But watch yourself, or you also may be tempted. Carry each other's burdens, and in this way you will fulfill the law of Christ.

This passage is the first reference we mention that comes from the NT letters. In many ways the sheer volume of material in the letters about relationships is itself a strong argument for the centrality of relationships in God's plan for his people. A close examination might reveal that the letters deal with relationships more than any other subject. In view of what we have looked at already, this is not surprising.

Here and in several other texts, Scripture shows how central our relationships are to new life in Christ. As we often hear that the three key words in real estate are "location, location, location," perhaps we need to understand that the three key words in biblical study are "context, context, context." The phrase in verse 2 "carry each other's burdens" should be looked at first in context before other applications are made. In applying this approach, we see that the "burdens" are burdens produced by sin. Christians are to be so involved in each other's lives that they know what sins others are struggling to overcome. Then they are to actually come alongside others and help them carry those burdens to a place where they are dealt with.

The statement, "In this way, you will fulfill the law of Christ," is an interesting one. "Law" in the New Testament does not always refer to a commandment or a code, but often to a "principle" (see Romans 7:21 and 8:2 for examples). Thus it would seem that helping your brother or sister to overcome a sin is a fulfillment of the principle of Christ. When we consider that the burden Jesus carried for us was our sin (Isaiah 53:4–6, 1 Peter 2:24), this conclusion makes good sense.

So relationships are at the center of God's will because it is in these relationships, that are anything but superficial, where we are fulfilling the very principle of Christ. We are following in his steps—not just by being a nice person who donates money or gives a ride to the doctor—but by being so involved in the lives of others that we are able to help them bear the burden of sin.

5. Philippians 1:27, 2:1–4

> Whatever happens, conduct yourselves in a manner worthy of the gospel of Christ. Then, whether I come and see you or only hear about you in my absence, I will know that you stand firm in one spirit, contending as one man for the faith of the gospel. (Philippians 1:27)

> If you have any encouragement from being united with Christ, if any comfort from his love, if any fellowship with the Spirit, if any tenderness and compassion, then make my joy complete by being like-minded, having the same love, being one in spirit and purpose. Do nothing out of selfish ambition or vain conceit, but in humility consider others better than yourselves. Each of you should look not only to your own interests, but also to the interests of others. (Philippians 2:1–4)

We expect that many will read the phrase "a manner worthy of the gospel" and think it refers to being moral, reading the Bible, attending church or having a sweet spirit. However, again, we must pay careful attention to the context. In these verses that follow, "the life worthy of the gospel" is described as standing firm in one spirit while having a deep unity with each other (1:27) and having a deep involvement in each other's concerns (2:4).

The life that is worthy of the gospel is a life that shows the gospel at work in our relationships. The same point is made in the letter to the Ephesians. Paul begins chapter 4, "As a prisoner for the Lord, then, I urge you to live a life worthy of the calling you have received." What is the rest of the chapter about? Relationships. Particularly notice the two verses that follow his admonition:

> Be completely humble and gentle; be patient, bearing with one another in love. Make every effort to keep the unity of the Spirit through the bond of peace. (4:2–3)

It is as though Paul is consistently echoing in his letters what Jesus said in John 13:34–35 (though John had not yet recorded these words in writing, they no doubt were well known).

Relationships are at the center of God's will because this is the way you live a life worthy of the gospel and of the Lord.

6. 1 John 1:7–9

> But if we walk in the light, as he is in the light, we have fellowship with one another, and the blood of Jesus, his Son, purifies us from all sin. If we claim to be without sin, we deceive ourselves and the truth is not in us. If we confess our sins, he is faithful and just and will forgive us our sins and purify us from all unrighteousness.

In the letter of 1 John a great contrast is drawn between living in the light and living in the darkness. But what does it mean to "walk in the light"? Again consider the context. We would argue that it is parallel to verse nine and that "walking in the light" and "confessing our sins" are what someone has called the Siamese twins of 1 John.

Walking in the light is living our lives with openness and transparency in response to the blood of Christ. Fellowship (*koinonia*) is so important because it is both the practice and the product of walking in the light and living in the light—light that is produced by the cross of Christ.

So how central are our relationships to following Jesus?

1. Coupled with loving God.
2. How we show we are disciples.
3. Something to be devoted to as we come into Christ.
4. How we fulfill the principle of Christ.
5. How we live a life worthy of the gospel and the Lord.
6. Where walking in the light leads.

Whenever you think: "I need to get serious about my relationship with God," do you immediately realize that means, "I have got to get serious about my relationships with other believers"? We have not included all the material we could have examined, but these key texts show us that there is no doubt that God sees relationships with our brothers and sisters in Christ at the center of the target.

Make no mistake, none of this is arbitrary. Everything about God's plan is purposeful. We were made for relationships. The very nature of God is at stake here. There is one God, but he is Father and Son and Holy Spirit—by nature there is relationship. Jesus makes that abundantly clear throughout the gospel of John (for example see 3:35, 5:19–20, 14:26, 17:2).

How can we ignore the centrality of our relationships as we

worship and serve a God who in his very nature demonstrates relationships to us? They are the fulfillment of the kingdom of God in the midst of human culture. We find richness in life not in gadgets, cars or houses, but in relationships—first with God and then with one another. But not only do we find fullness, but we find transformation, which we will see as we move on.

Making It Real

1. How does a relationship with God go hand in hand with relationships with each other? In other words, how does the first lead to the second, and how does the second have impact on the first?

2. Look back to the answers you wrote down after the Introduction. In light of what was discussed here in chapter 1, what thoughts do you have about these questions and your answers? What action do you want to take?

3. If you do not see yourself as a relationship person naturally, what changes in your thinking do you need to be open to making?

4. What responsibility do the ideas in this chapter give us regarding our friends who believe they have a good relationship with God without deep connection to other people? Do you think you know such people?

Relationships According to God's Grace

Unless we decide to be a hermit, relationships will be an important part of our lives. Contact and connection with other human beings is not only necessary for conducting business and accomplishing many tasks, but also for enjoying life. Only a rare few do not feel an innate desire to be in some sort of social setting, be it a family, a poker group, a club or a team. We have fishing and golfing buddies, shopping buddies, support groups or even bars like the one in the old television series *Cheers*, "where everybody knows your name." One way or another most people find a way to have relationships.

However, like most everything else in life we can carry on our relationships, in Paul's words, "according to worldly wisdom," or we can conduct them according to God's wisdom (see Paul's discussion of this in 1 Corinthians 1–3). In his second letter to the Corinthians Paul specifically mentions these two different ways you can approach relationships both within and without the spiritual family. Look at his statement:

> Now this is our boast: Our conscience testifies that we have conducted ourselves in the world, and especially in our relations with you, in the holiness and sincerity that are from God. We have done so not according to worldly wisdom but according to God's grace. (2 Corinthians 1:12)

Correction and Example Needed

In his first letter to this church Paul noted that their relationships were anything but godly. Though they were disciples of Christ, their faith was at a dangerous place. The list of their relationship issues was shocking:

- They were divided into cliquish groups following certain leaders: chapters 1–3.
- They had become arrogant in their relationship with Paul: chapter 4:18–19.
- Some were taking each other to court with lawsuits: chapter 6.
- Some were thinking they could abrogate their marriage vows and leave their spouses just because they were not Christians: chapter 7.
- Some people were exercising their right to eat meat without being concerned about offending someone else's conscience. Instead, some acted puffed up and prideful: chapter 8.
- Some acted insensitively toward the poorer members by not waiting on each other at the Lord's Supper (which in that time would have been a common meal also). Also some were getting drunk—not recognizing the body of the Lord nor the fellowship of the church: chapter 11.
- Then, there was the whole pride-based controversy about who had the greatest gift, in a spirit of selfish competition: chapters 12–14.

To such a church Paul not only wanted to bring teaching to correct these issues, but he wanted to show them with his own life a whole different way of conducting relationships. He wanted to show them the difference between relationships lived out according to the world's wisdom and those lived out according to God's grace (2 Corinthians 1:12). If you compare Paul's language in 1 Corinthians 1–3 with this passage, you will notice a slight difference in the contrast he draws there and here.

In the 1 Corinthians passage, the contrast is between "the world's wisdom" and "God's wisdom." In the other passage it is between "the world's wisdom" and "God's grace" (see Figure 3). What we should, no doubt, understand is that living according to God's wisdom means living according to God's grace.

Figure 3

1 Corinthians 1-3	2 Corinthians 1
The world's wisdom	The world's wisdom
God's wisdom	God's grace

Relationships that are conducted according to the world's wisdom will always have some element of "self" in mind—certainly some more than others, but it will always be there. Relationships conducted according to God's grace will be conducted with two things in mind: God's grace to us and our need to pass grace on to others. The kingdom has come to us through the extravagant generosity of God. That fact now stands at the center of all our relationships.

In View of God's Mercy

Let me (Tom) tell you what helped me to understand this extravagant generosity of God. Thirty-five years ago, my bride of four years and I took a vacation to a remote part of Colorado. We settled in a little house trailer at the bottom of a mountain. Just after daybreak, as Sheila slept in, I got up and hiked to the top of a peak in the Wet Mountains.

Reaching the top, I found my breath taken away by a spectacular view. From that vantage point I could see most of the

Sangre de Cristo mountain range across the valley. I would later learn this was a series of more than twenty 14,000-foot peaks, and it seemed they stretched as far as I could see from the east to the west. (To see it for yourself check out this Web site: http://www.sangrespanorama.com.)

I had my copy of the New International Version of the New Testament which had just been released a few months before. In this fresh new translation I read these words from Romans 12:1:

> Therefore, I urge you, brothers, in view of God's mercy, to offer your bodies as living sacrifices, holy and pleasing to God—this is your spiritual act of worship.

With that spectacular view of the Sangre de Cristo range (which by the way is translated "The Blood of Christ"), I thought about how the book of Romans is really a series of 14,000-foot theological peaks describing again and again the mercy and grace of God in towering terms. And what I came to realize is that I need to live my whole life never losing sight of that spectacular view of God's mercy. I especially need to conduct all my relationships with that view as the backdrop.

One of my favorite pictures of the Sangre de Cristo range is one in which you can see the little town of Westcliffe sitting in the valley dwarfed by those majestic mountains. As I type this, that framed photo hangs directly in front of me above my computer screen. It was many years after I was there that I looked at that photo and realized that the church is really like that little town. We are the community of God, with our "town" built at the foot of the towering, majestic mountains of God's abundant grace. Just as you can do very little in Westcliffe without seeing those mountains rising above you, so we must conduct all our relationships—in and out of the church—with a clear view of the mercy of God, always allowing that view to shape and control our relationships.

This means more than being superficially nice to each other. A close look at God's grace reveals much about what should be involved in relationships. In the rest of this book we will look at some of the key texts that describe our involvement with "one another." In each case what God calls us to be for one another is rooted in what God is for us as he shows us his grace. In other words, there is nothing arbitrary about the "one another" passages. He did not just randomly pick out a dozen things for us to do. No, they all are theologically based in the character of God and in his dynamic with us in which we receive his grace. Look at several examples.

Making It Clear
- In Romans 12, after calling us to live our lives with God's mercy in view, Paul soon tells us that we belong to one another (v5). The world's wisdom teaches us to be independent, to come and go as we please. And so in much religion you see a huge buy-in to that philosophy.

    However, as we look seriously at the grace of God, we see that the only one who could have been truly independent and did not need a thing was God, and yet in his grace he came to be with us and belong to us. So speaking of Jesus in Philippians 2, Paul says he did not count equality with God something to be grasped, but he emptied himself and took the form of a servant. And who was he serving? He was serving us, and the word *doulos* means "bond servant," one who belongs to the one he serves.

    We who are in Christ are blessed today because God did not remain independent of us, but came in Christ, humbled himself and became one of us, and belonged to us. If God has treated us this way, what should we do? Surely it means to embrace the idea that we belong to each other. By the grace of God we have been brought into the same family to serve one another.

- Reading on in Romans 12, we soon see the call for us to be "devoted to one another" (v10). The word *philostorgos* speaks of the kind of commitment one has to friends and family members, whom one cares for deeply. When we see the grace of God, we see one who brings us into his circle of friends (John 15:13–15). We see one who adopts us into his family (Hebrews 2:11). We see one who vows he will never leave us or forsake us (Hebrews 13:5). God, in his grace, becomes the model of how we are to commit ourselves to one another.

- In Colossians 3:16 and Ephesians 4:15 we have a different type of "one another" passage. Here we are called to admonish one another and speak the truth in love to one another. How is this way of relating to others "according to God's grace"? For some people grace means just overlooking faults and sins. Their view of grace is that we should be soft on sin. For them, to speak to someone else about his or her sin is to be without grace or mercy.

    But what do we see when we look at God, who is always rich in mercy and full of grace? We see a father who knows what sin does to us and who admonishes and speaks truth to us. And now he calls us to do this for one another. Those who live according to the world's wisdom both within and without churches, usually take one of three options: (1) They just ignore a problem. (2) They gossip about it to others. (3) They blast a person with the truth. None of those actions show grace. Grace gets involved. Grace cares. Grace speaks truth but in ways that show love.

- For a number of years the two of us have been involved with churches that have attempted to make relationships a high priority. In some cases, we have seen abuses occur where people began to "lord it over" others and seek an unhealthy control. People affected by such abuse will instinctively pull back from relationships out of fear. However, it is a mistake to try to correct this abuse with less commitment to one another and less involvement in each other's lives. The correction is found not in less interest in each other but in conducting our relationships according to the grace of God.

Making It Real

1. Carefully think about how you are tempted to conduct your relationships in the world and with other believers according to the world's wisdom. Think about these areas and others: (1) business matters, (2) medical situations, (3) school or governmental interactions, (4) neighborhood issues, (5) relationship with your spouse, (6) relationship with your children, (7) relationship with church leaders, (8) relationship with those in your small group, (9) relationship with best friends.
2. Take a careful inventory of the ways God has treated you because of his grace.
3. What on your list strikes you as the one place where you need to relate to others "according to the grace of God"?
4. Were you able to check out this Web site I mentioned: http://www.sangrespanorama.com? What effect would it have on you if you could always be seeing the grace of God towering in the background of every relationship?

Loving One Another

> "A new command I give you: Love one another. As I have loved you, so you must love one another. By this all men will know that you are my disciples, if you love one another."
>
> John 13:34–35

Any discussion of "one another" passages really has to start and end with Jesus' "new" command (John 13:34) to "love one another." To "love one another" is by far the most frequent in a list of the "one another" passages—thirteen out of about fifty-nine by our count.

The force of the language demands attention as well: "You must love one another," Jesus says (John 13:34). He states it as a command. Then he follows with, "By this all men will know that you are my disciples, if you love one another." Paul says we have a "continuing debt to love one another" (Romans 13:8), and it is God himself who teaches us to "love one another" (1 Thessalonians 4:9, KJV). And the apostle John, sometimes called "the apostle of love," calls for it five times in 1 John 3 and 4. In fact, a story circulated in the early church saying that John so frequently repeated the injunction, "My little children, love one another," that his listeners grew tired of it and urged him to teach them something else. To which he supposedly replied, "My little children, love one another." If indeed this did happen, we do not think it was due to John's senility but to his conviction.

Familial Love

To help us grasp the nature and force of this love and how it should look as it is lived out in the fellowship, Scripture uses the powerful metaphor of the family. It is embedded in the fabric of the entire Bible. God is our Father. Jesus is the elder brother, the "firstborn" (Colossians 1:15, 18). We are "brothers" and "sisters." We are part of a "brotherhood" (*adelphotes*—1 Peter 2:17, 5:9). The word "brothers" is used 250 times in reference to Christians. We see the adoption motif in Ephesians 1:5. And thus follows the whole concept of being "born" or "reborn" into God's family. We are even blood brothers, according to Ephesians 1:7.

We are enjoined to "keep on loving each other as brothers" (Hebrews 13:1), and in Romans 12:10 Paul brings this family-style love to the forefront. The New International Version reads, "Be devoted to one another in brotherly love." We are familiar with the Greek word for "brotherly love"—*philadelphia*—because of the city in Pennsylvania that is referred to as "the city of brotherly love."

Paul goes beyond merely encouraging brotherly love by saying that we should be "devoted" to it. Here the Greek word refers to a "heartfelt love," from the bottom of your heart, as we might say. It transcends obligation—even that of a family member—and requires a depth of warmth, a concern and a loyalty that probably should characterize all families, though many, unfortunately, fall short.

The ultimate standard for understanding this love that is required of us is plainly stated: "As I have loved you, so you must love one another" (John 13:34b). Additionally, it is God's love that serves as the motivation for our love "since God so loved us, we also ought to love one another" (1 John 4:11).

Secure in God

In order to understand what this amazing love of Jesus is all about, let us go back and look at our original text in its context. The setting is the night before Jesus' death, and John gives us this intriguing story that is not found in the other Gospels. With none of the disciples looking for an opportunity to serve, Jesus himself—supposedly the one to be honored—stood up, found the basin and the towel, and went from person to person washing the disciples' dirty feet.

Were the disciples shocked at this? Probably not. Jesus was not doing something out of character. He had taught these stubborn position seekers to be humble and to serve, and then he had lived it. Now John says: "Having loved his own who were in the world, he now showed them the full extent of his love" (John 13:1b). The New American Standard Bible (NASB) is more likely a better translation: "Having loved His own who were in the world, He loved them to the end." All along Jesus had been serving them, and this continued to the end, even when his inner struggles intensified as the fateful hour drew near.

How do we maintain such a servant mentality toward those in our lives? How does a person who is leading overcome the fear of looking weak?

The answer most likely is found in verse 3: "Jesus knew that the Father had put all things under his power, and that he had come from God and was returning to God." Being secure in his identity freed Jesus to focus on the needs of others. We should be able to tie this truth to the previous chapter in this book. Conducting our relationships according to God's grace means conducting them with the security that our identity comes from God's grace.

So many strange and hurtful things are done in relationships because people are acting out of their insecurities. Knowing we have our security from God alone sets us free to love and serve with abandon.

Loving Means Serving

When we look at this passage as a whole we see something striking: to love someone is to serve them—that is, meet their needs. Love is not an abstract thought. It is not a passing emotion. It is not a benevolent inclination. Love is an action. It is something that is demonstrated. In this instance it involves time, water, a towel and knees on a hard floor.

Do you love your brother in Christ; your sister? Careful now. It will almost always involve time. Are you hoarding yours? It may also involve such varied things as patience, forgiveness, gasoline, a lawn mower and sweat. Or how about changing diapers (literally or spiritually), sacrificing something you really like, listening, running up your cell phone minutes. We say, "I just really love that brother." Do we? Is there action? Is it shown?

I (Tom) have discovered something about myself, and I wish it were not true. In general I like to serve people, but there are certain people I am not as excited about serving as I am others. I would not have thought this was true, except when teaching on this topic several months back, I noticed that there were certain phone calls I was returning promptly and others I was not. It struck me that returning a phone call is an act of serving and loving—it shows respect for the needs of others. I saw in my reluctance or procrastination a clear lack of love. If you had asked me if I loved these people, my words would not have lined up with my actions.

I brought this into the light with the whole church and have since seen some real change. But now aware of this tendency, I need to be vigilant about having the right heart. The call to love is the call to act, and not just to act if my own emotions are gratified.

The call to love is carefully qualified: Jesus says,

> "You call me 'Teacher' and 'Lord,' and rightly so, for that is what I am. Now that I, your Lord and Teacher, have washed your feet, you also should wash one another's feet. I have set you an example that you should do as I have done for you." (John 13:13–15)

And then in v34: "As I have loved you, so you must love one another."

We said in the first sentence of this study that the New Testament is a radical book. We are not called to volunteer a small amount of reluctant service to this poor little charity called the church so we can assuage some of our guilt. We are called to be inspired by Jesus to give ourselves just as he did among this body of believers called the family of God. How do you suppose he washed those feet? What did his body language communicate? Did the disciples feel from him "I would really rather not be here"? We are called to imitate him in heart and attitude as we do the things that our brothers and sisters most need.

Open Our Eyes to Needs

In a crowded room of hungry men who were no doubt confused by the events rapidly taking place, Jesus was aware of what the group needed. To really love we must pray that God will open our eyes and make us aware. Many opportunities to serve and show love slip by us because we are focused on what happened to us (i.e., "I can't believe he did that."), what is happening to us (i.e., "I have got so much to do.") or what could happen to us (i.e., "I might lose my job.").

Often awareness of the needs of others is present in our lives to the extent that we are finding our security in God. Imagine how the person who has confidence and security from God would be freed from all the "happenings"—past, present and future—and be free to open his or her eyes and be aware of the needs of others.

Just as there were two great commandments on which hung all the law and the prophets, we can easily say that this is the great NT commandment on which hangs every other "one another" exhortation or command that we will examine in this book. Everything else in this book describes an expression of the love we are to have for other people.

Are we moved and compelled by the love of Jesus? Do we want to love one another the way he loved? Do we want to do that, whatever it takes? This is a decision it would be good to make before you read on.

Making It Real

1. Is there anything about serving that you find distasteful or repugnant? Be honest and then think about it in light of Jesus.
2. Can you see in your life any connection between getting your identity from God and loving and serving other people?
3. How can you become more aware of the needs of others or the needs of the group? What will you do with this awareness?

Accepting One Another

The more time we spend thinking about our relationships with each other, the more we are impressed with the New Testament's teaching about the kind of relationships we need to have. It is so incredibly practical. It is like a primer on Christian relationships. Actually, it is *the* primer on Christian relationships. We have got to put these truths into practice in our lives! Not only because God said it, and but because it really works.

Two Extremes: Judgment and Apathy
In our struggle to be "Christian" in our dealings with each other, we seem to repeatedly fall into one of two extremes: either a hard-line, judgmental rejection of anything that is not just like "us," or an open-ended acceptance of just about anyone or anything. In Romans 15 Paul takes us beyond "nice words" and brings us down to earth: "Accept one another, then, just as Christ accepted you, in order to bring praise to God" (Romans 15:7).

In the churches of both our childhoods there was a tendency toward the judgmental side of things. We grew up with a fairly rigid view of what was right and what was wrong. Therefore people were accepted or rejected because they held certain views or beliefs. We pretty much had a checklist. Passages like Luke 7:36–50 where Jesus accepts the embarrassing display by a "sinful" woman were somewhat difficult, as we tended to feel a little more sympathetic to the attitude of the host, Simon the Pharisee.

So for some of us Paul's challenge is very revolutionary, especially as we meditate on the "just as Christ accepted you" part of the verse. How exactly did Christ accept us? If we are honest with ourselves, we have to admit that we did not have it all together then or even now. At best, as someone said, we are "works in progress," and the reality is that no matter how hard we try, we are a mess and in need of a bunch of grace.

Accused or Excused

Many years ago I (Steve) heard someone say that there are two kinds of people in the world: the "accused" and the "excused." It resonated with me, perhaps because I was definitely one of the accused ones. I tend to feel guilty, to beat myself up about my faults—to struggle, in general, to accept "me" as God does. And if you cannot relate, then you may be one of the excused ones who tend to think everything is someone else's fault.

There is something very profound here that takes us back to the very nature of God himself. We need to understand that the God of Scripture is a patient God, a longsuffering God, a Father who longs for us to come back home, who runs to meet us when we are still a long way off. We need to accept his acceptance so we can pass it on to others.

So for the church to be the "body of Christ" on this earth we must drink in deeply this aspect of God's heart. We must learn to be accepting as he is accepting. We have to put to death every hint of the judgmental and pharisaical attitudes that hide in our heart and learn to accept others, to embrace others, to welcome others into our lives and homes and churches.

The Romans 15:7 text also tells us that this kind of heart, this kind of attitude, this way of relating to others has a striking result—praise being given to God.

This is a good thing. It is not an easy thing.

Maybe everything in you is screaming out that God is also a just God who hates evil and that in the Old Testament he often brought his judgment down on people who did wrong. So how does it all fit together?

Conviction and Acceptance

We have actually just looked at one verse of a whole section of Romans where Paul is dealing with this very question. How do we blend having deep convictions with an equally deep level of acceptance?

Let us start with Romans 14:1: "Accept him whose faith is weak, without passing judgment on disputable matters." This discussion runs on down through 15:7: "Accept one another, then, just as Christ accepted you, in order to bring praise to God."

Why does Paul have to say this, much less repeat it?

Because we really need to hear it twice! In the following verses, Paul applies this concept to a practice that was putting the brothers into quite a turmoil. Evidently it was a common pagan practice to kill animals for sacrifice to the "gods" and then sell the meat that was not burned in a nearby meat market. Some of the brothers had no problem with eating this meat, while others were horrified at the idea of eating meat that had been offered to an idol. (See 1 Corinthians 8 and 10:14–33 for more on this issue.)

The surprising thing about this passage, especially to someone from a judgmental background, is that Paul does not get into a discussion about who was right and who was wrong.

Interestingly enough, he does indicate that those with "weak faith" are the ones who have a conviction that eating the meat is wrong. You may think, "But I thought that if you had convictions about right and wrong you were 'strong.'" We all still have a lot to learn about the way God sees things. Let's keep looking at this…

Paul adds another first-century issue in verses 5 and 6 of Romans 14: is it okay to treat one day as more special to worship God than other days? (Perhaps we could think Christmas and Easter in Western culture.) Again Paul doesn't belabor the "who's right" issue. He focuses on accepting others as brothers. The bottom-line principle is and always will be love, and what Paul is saying is that love means accepting our brothers, "warts and all."

Respect Others' Convictions

It is important to note that Paul says he is talking about "disputable matters" in Romans 14:1. These are not the seven unifying elements of Christianity that he lays out in Ephesians 4. Still we have to recognize the importance of deep personal convictions even in this disputable matter. See what he says in verse 5:

> One man considers one day more sacred than another; another man considers every day alike. Each one should be fully convinced in his own mind. (Romans 14:5)

In fact Paul feels so strongly about this that he says in verse 23 that to go against our conviction is "sin," even if the conviction is misguided.

There are a series of great questions in these verses:

- Who are you to judge someone else's servant? (v4)
- Why do you judge your brother? (v10)

- Why do you look down on your brother? (v10)

We have two basic struggles with each other: judging and prejudice, which is prejudging. So, perhaps it is really only one struggle. Paul hits the judging angle pretty hard here, and James drives home a related point about prejudice in James 2:1–9 (Holman CSB):

> My brothers, as believers in our glorious Lord Jesus Christ, don't show favoritism. Suppose a man comes into your meeting wearing a gold ring and fine clothes, and a poor man in shabby clothes also comes in. If you show special attention to the man wearing fine clothes and say, "Here's a good seat for you," but say to the poor man, "You stand there" or "Sit on the floor by my feet," have you not discriminated among yourselves and become judges with evil thoughts?
>
> Listen, my dear brothers: Has not God chosen those who are poor in the eyes of the world to be rich in faith and to inherit the kingdom he promised those who love him? But you have insulted the poor. Is it not the rich who are exploiting you? Are they not the ones who are dragging you into court? Are they not the ones who are slandering the noble name of him to whom you belong?
>
> If you really keep the royal law found in Scripture, "Love your neighbor as yourself," you are doing right. But if you show favoritism, you sin and are convicted by the law as lawbreakers.

Prejudice can be based on many differences—not just socioeconomic as we see here, but cultural and racial as well. We may look around and congratulate ourselves on our diversity.

And if we individually and collectively are by choice in relationships that show diversity, we should be glad. But that does not mean that we have it all figured out. We always must be aware of the pitfalls and keep working to improve our relationships regardless of "cash," color or culture. This is why what Paul writes next in Romans 14 is so powerful:

> For we will all stand before God's judgment seat. It is written:
>
> "'As surely as I live,' says the Lord,
> 'every knee will bow before me;
> every tongue will confess to God.'"
>
> So then, each of us will give an account of himself to God. Therefore let us stop passing judgment on one another. (Romans 14:10–13)

Paul says that the answer to these questions needs to be made in light of the day when all will face God's judgment. There will be no "I'm right" or "you're wrong" on that day. We will all face God. No finger-pointing. His "rightness" will be perfectly obvious to all. And in light of this we need to "stop passing judgment on one another," which is actually the same thing as "accepting one another." Here the Holman CSB reads: "Let us no longer criticize one another." That seems to hit closer to home. And, of course, let us not play semantic games: "I'm not judging. I'm just pointing out their faults."

The point of our discussion here is not to delve into the theological issues that separate us, but to focus on the practical aspects of how we accept our brothers. Paul makes it clear: we are to accept others as Christ accepted us.

Of course, there is something in me (Steve) that wants to qualify it, that wants to explain it, that wants to post conditions and regulations. Maybe that is just me, or maybe you deal with this temptation too. However, Paul says simply to accept each other. No "ifs," "ands" or "buts." Accept. Our job is to lock in on the accepting. Let us try to focus on that, and let the other issues take care of themselves.

Greet One Another

One of the ways the New Testament illustrates the importance of this concept is by the frequent use of the term "greet." Greeting seems to be a pretty important aspect of relationships: it occurs twenty-seven times as a command and sixty-eight in all its grammatical forms. Let's limit ourselves to looking at the "greet one another" passages. There are four of them.

- Romans 16:16—Greet one another with a holy kiss. All the churches of Christ send greetings.
- 1 Corinthians 16:20—All the brothers here send you greetings. Greet one another with a holy kiss.
- 2 Corinthians 13:12—Greet one another with a holy kiss.
- 1 Peter 5:14—Greet one another with a kiss of love. Peace to all of you who are in Christ.

We would suggest that the importance of greeting is evident because of the repetition. Perhaps the reference to the holy kiss is somewhat strange to those in the United States where a handshake (or a hug) is generally the preferred greeting. Again, the emphasis must be on the heart behind it, which we see in the emphasis on a "holy" kiss or by Peter's "kiss of love." Greeting with a kiss remains a common practice in Europe and much of South America.

Honestly, it took us (Steve and Diane) living in Argentina to get used to the practice. Just like a handshake, various levels of warmth and acceptance can also be communicated with a perfunctory kiss on the cheek. Because of the possibility of ungodly levels of excitement, in some instances we have the repeated injunction to keep the greetings "holy." We experience the exact same things with our practice of embracing in the fellowship.

As we think about accepting one another, the two of us (Steve and Tom) have discussed that such acceptance does not mean a whole lot or does not positively affect a relationship unless the other person feels it. For example, Joe may say "I accept Ernesto." But if Ernesto does not see and hear things that make him feel accepted, doubts will remain in his heart.

Perhaps this is one place that greeting and accepting connect, with warm affectionate greetings being ways of helping the other person feel the reality of our acceptance of them.

We don't believe that it is the kind of greeting—hug, kiss or handshake—that is the issue. The challenge for all of us is to really communicate the heart of love and acceptance that must, according to these NT writings, be a part of our interaction in the church.

Making It Real

1. How does your background, religious or otherwise, affect your ability to be accepting of differences in other people?
2. Do you see yourself as being more of an "accused" personality or an "excused" one? How do others see you? How does this affect your acceptance of others?
3. Identify two or three people that you have a hard time "accepting." Will you be comfortable saying, "God, judge me just as I judge them"?
4. Why should you give more emphasis to the quality of your greetings?

5
Belonging to One Another

As we examine the biblical teaching about relationships, their centrality in God's plan and their basis in the Word, we may be struck by the dichotomy between God's standard and our own personal experience. We see that biblical principles on relationships are countercultural and even to some degree counterintuitive (more on that later). We may find it all somewhat overwhelming. Concepts such as "perfectly united in mind and thought" seem altogether unattainable. Or "that all of them may be one, Father, just as you are in me and I am in you" seems to be another lofty, inaccessible ambition. Maybe you are thinking, "I'd like to have these kinds of relationships, but my schedule, my kids' activities, my health—how is it going to work?"

The other track we have taken in this book is to call us to put into practice what we are hearing. This "putting into practice" was one of the things that really impacted me when I (Steve) first became associated with the fellowship of churches I am now with. From my background I was accustomed to a strong emphasis on biblical teaching, so the teaching on relationships was not new to me. What surprised me was how diligently people implemented the teaching and how radically their lives were changed. In seeing this, I was convicted to my core.

So what we (Tom and Steve) have seen even in our lifetime is that churches and movements go through times of turmoil that often cause us to reexamine every aspect of our faith. When this happens, some of us tend to become critical and suspicious—perhaps even jaded in our attitude toward the message bearer and even to the message itself. We can become less responsive and obedient to what the Bible calls us to do. Yet, if we do not apply it, the information we receive does us no real good. (See James 1:22–25.)

We Belong to Each Other

Our focus in this chapter comes from Romans 12:5, "belonging to one another," but let us think first about how this verse fits into the context of the whole book of Romans. The book is essentially a presentation of the gospel, the good news and God's power for salvation, according to Paul (Romans 1:16). In chapters 1–3 he points out that the Gentile and the Jew, in fact all of us, are lost without this good news, and Paul details in subsequent chapters how we attain this salvation by faith (4–5) through baptism (6) and by the help of God's Spirit (8). He lays out in chapters 9–11 the thorny issue of the Jewish rejection of the gospel in light of God's desire and his own passion for the Jews to be saved. It all comes to a powerful conclusion in 11:33–36 (Holman CSB):

> Oh, the depth of the riches
> both of the wisdom and the knowledge of God!
> How unsearchable His judgments
> and untraceable His ways!
> For who has known the mind of the Lord?
> Or who has been His counselor?
> Or who has ever first given to Him,
> and has to be repaid?

> For from Him and through Him and to Him are all things.
> To Him be the glory forever. Amen.

Based on this astounding grace (Romans 12:1–2) Paul sums up the Christian life in terms of being a living sacrifice. After stating this he immediately turns his attention to how we function together as part of the body of Christ. Much in contrast with so much preaching through the centuries and today, the focus in the New Testament is primarily on the corporate nature of our Christian experience.

Watch for Self-Focused Thinking

Paul starts by telling us to think about ourselves sensibly ("with sober judgment" NIV), to not think more highly of ourselves than we should. Now this is the countercultural and counterintuitive aspect that we mentioned earlier. Everything in our society and even within us screams: "I'm numero uno!" "It is all about me!" But Paul evidently saw this type of attitude as a significant problem in our relationships, and he mentioned it first.

So, what do you think? What does our independent or self-focused thinking sound like?

- "I'll attend if it is convenient for me."
- "I'm too busy."
- "I don't feel connected."
- "I can't afford to give too much time."

How does this thinking affect us? One, we do not function as a part of the church. And two, we do not use our gifts that Paul specifically talks about here for the church. We take them and use them for our own benefit, for our own personal profit. Paul chooses one of his favorite analogies to help us understand this:

the church as a body. Actually, in his first letter to the Corinthians he goes into much more detail to explain this analogy, perhaps due to the immaturity of the Corinthian church. Let us look at some of the more pertinent parts of 1 Corinthians 12 in The Message Bible for impact:

> 12–13a: You can easily enough see how this kind of thing works by looking no further than your own body. Your body has many parts—limbs, organs, cells—but no matter how many parts you can name, you're still one body. It's exactly the same with Christ. By means of his one Spirit, we all said good-bye to our partial and piecemeal lives. We each used to independently call our own shots, but then we entered into a large and integrated life in which he has the final say in everything.
>
> 19–24: But I also want you to think about how this keeps your significance from getting blown up into self-importance. For no matter how significant you are, it is only because of what you are a part of. An enormous eye or a gigantic hand wouldn't be a body, but a monster. What we have is one body with many parts, each its proper size and in its proper place. No part is important on its own. Can you imagine Eye telling Hand, "Get lost; I don't need you"? Or, Head telling Foot, "You're fired; your job has been phased out"? As a matter of fact, in practice it works the other way—the "lower" the part, the more basic, and therefore necessary. You can live without an eye, for instance, but not without a stomach. When it's a part of your own body you are concerned with, it makes no difference whether the part is visible or clothed, higher or lower. You give it dignity and honor just as it is, without comparisons. If anything, you

have more concern for the lower parts than the higher. If you had to choose, wouldn't you prefer good digestion to full-bodied hair?
25-26: The way God designed our bodies is a model for understanding our lives together as a church: every part dependent on every other part, the parts we mention and the parts we don't, the parts we see and the parts we don't. If one part hurts, every other part is involved in the hurt, and in the healing. If one part flourishes, every other part enters into the exuberance.
27: You are Christ's body—that's who you are! You must never forget this. Only as you accept your part of that body does your "part" mean anything.

This is such an illuminating passage and should help us to understand the main points of this chapter: We belong to each other. We are connected. It is not about me. It is about us! The truth is we cannot function as God desires without each other.

Members of One Another

In looking back at verses 4 and 5 of Romans 12, we see as well that there are many parts, there are many functions, there are many members, but all in one body. Paul calls us to be members of one another ("each member belongs to all the others" NIV). I belong to you. You belong to me. We belong to each other.

Your role in the body is determined by: (1) the measure of faith God has given you, and (2) the gifts God has given you. What does "the measure of faith" mean? There are two ways to look at it: subjectively (i.e., my function in the body is according to the personal amount of faith I have) or objectively (i.e., my function in the body is purely dependent upon my trust in God to use me). There is not a huge difference in how either works out as we live every day because we must trust God to use us, and we are only limited by our faith that he will do so.

Do you believe that God put you here and gave you the exact things necessary for you to accomplish in the church what he intends? The gifts are based on grace, according to the text. In other words, we have done nothing to deserve them or earn them, or even claim that they are ours alone. Because we belong to the body, the gifts we have belong to the body as well.

In verses 6–8 a variety of gifts are mentioned: prophecy, service, teaching, exhorting ("encouraging" NIV), giving ("contributing to the needs of others" NIV), leading and showing mercy. There has been much discussion through the years about the nature of the gifts, to what degree Paul is talking about "spiritual gifts" that were limited to the first century, or whether some of the gifts continue to function more like talents or abilities. We will not delve into a study of the spiritual gifts because it is beyond the scope of our topic. What we can know is that God has "gifted" all of us with ways to build up the body.

Interestingly Gene Getz in his book *Building Up One Another*[1] points out that nowhere in the New Testament does it tell us to "search for" or "try to discover" what our gift is. He shares that for years he taught and encouraged members of his church to focus on this "gift-based ministry" idea. He found that instead of producing the body function that Paul is talking about here, the focus on discovering gifts produced frustration in mature Christians who seemed unable to identify their gifts and produced fixation in people who were determined to use their gift to the exclusion of all else or even to the detriment of those

---

1. Gene A. Getz, *Building Up One Another* (Colorado Springs: Chariot Victor Publishing, 2002), 9–19.

in the fellowship. He found that by focusing on helping people mature—to use their strengths and at the same time to work on their weaknesses—that greater unity and maturity was developed in the church.

At any rate, Paul's teaching is directed toward how to use the gifts, not how to figure out what they are. Again our point: we need to focus on being part of the body, being a member, belonging. What can you do today to express that you belong to the body and to help someone else feel they belong as well?

Paul's teaching on relationships in Romans is not limited to chapter 12; it continues throughout the rest of the book. I think it is of special interest to see in this context the strength of Paul's language in Romans 15:1–2:

> We who are strong ought to bear with the failings of the weak and not to please ourselves. Each of us should please his neighbor for his good, to build him up.

Although the NIV uses the phrase "ought to," the Holman CSB uses the stronger expression, "we have an obligation to." Why? It goes back to the essence of what we are talking about: We belong to one another. We are members of one another. And that implies obligation. It means that we do not seek to please ourselves, but rather seek to please our neighbor (15:2–3). This is the example that Jesus set for us.

"Pleasing" here is not in the context of satisfying a whim, but in the context of helping others do well spiritually. Paul is talking about the weak and the strong and he is talking about things that would cause your brother to stumble, that might hurt him spiritually. Obviously, this can be taken out of context and wrongly used to get people to do all kinds of things for you. That was not Paul's point. He is discussing a mutual obligation to each other.

As we close we want to come back to something that we have all experienced at one time or another: we want to feel like we belong, that we are part of something. God has designed the church, his body, to meet that need.

This is our heart: "Thank you, God! Thank you, church! I need you. You need me. We need each other."

Making It Real

1. Are you functioning as part of a local body of Christians? How? What do you contribute to the daily working of your church?

2. How do you see your need to connect?

3. How does your own feeling about yourself affect the way you interact in the fellowship? What can you do to improve?

4. Who in the body is involved in your life? Take the time to express to them how much you appreciate them and how much you need them.

Teaching and Admonishing One Another

One of the unique characteristics of Christian relationships is the aspect of having responsibility for another person. Like almost anything else, this can be taken to an unhealthy extreme, but there is no question from the Scriptures that God intended for us to be aware of the lives and needs of others and to be responsible for giving them input, counsel and guidance. And, of course, to expect the same from them toward us.

Two Extremes

Let us address two issues that may cause some of us to hesitate at this point. First, for those of us who were raised with the concept of "mind your own business" or have gravitated to that view because of the comfort it offers, we must be prepared to let God transform our thinking. Following God's plan, none of us will become busybodies, injecting ourselves obnoxiously into others' lives (2 Thessalonians 3:11, 1 Timothy 5:13). However, we will see that offering guidance, instruction, cautions, warnings and occasionally something even stronger is all a part of being faithful in our relationships.

Second, there are those who seem to know one Scripture better than any other: "Judge not, that ye be not judged" (Matthew 7:1, KJV). This injunction is often taken as an all-encompassing command not to involve ourselves in others' affairs. It is interesting to us that people who quote this passage may still do lots of judging. However, they do not share their thoughts with the people they judge; they share them with others.

In context, Jesus is condemning self-righteous judging, where we are unwilling to examine the issues in our own lives, but want to point out the wrongs in others' lives. He even goes on to tell us how we can handle our observations in a way that enables us to help our brother with issues in his life.

What we will see in this chapter is that we must care enough about each other to help each other to grow. And yet, we will look at what we suspect is the most neglected of all the "one another" concepts, even among fellowships committed to one-another relationships. The two of us are a part of such a church and know this to be the case where we are. It is also our guess that the one-another applications we will talk about in this chapter are among the ones most feared by even committed disciples.

As we look at the New Testament we will see that there is no "live and let live" view of life in the body of Christ, and yet many of us fear to challenge that widely-held cultural rule. At the same time some of us will feel reluctant about the content of this chapter because we have seen some of these ideas abused, and we allow the danger of abuse to cause us to pull back altogether. However, since it is so critical that we practice all aspects of involvement with one another, let us summon up our faith, pray for courage, be prepared to change and plunge in to see what the Scriptures say to us about teaching and admonishing each other.

Teaching One Another

To the Christians in Colosse Paul wrote these words:

> Let the word of Christ richly dwell within you, with all wisdom teaching and admonishing one another with psalms and hymns and spiritual songs, singing with thankfulness in your hearts to God. (Colossians 3:16, NASB)

The word translated "teaching" is the word *didasko*. Its meaning is rather plain and unambiguous. It means "to give instruction, to impart information or wisdom." It can be used, as it is today, in business, philosophy, spirituality, the arts and dozens of other areas. A parent may teach a child to cook, to fish, to manage money. An instructor may teach you to play the guitar. A coach may teach you to shoot a jump shot.

In this context, it is clear that Christians are to teach one another those things that will result in spiritual development and growth. One may teach another how to study the Bible or how to pray. We may be mentored and taught to more effectively share our faith. We may teach or be taught principles for overcoming temptation and besetting sins. Thinking of the subject of this book, you may teach someone how to conduct godly relationships. The list of possibilities is endless. Often the teaching is informal. We may simply pass on to someone something we have learned in a recent study time that we believe will help them as well.

In this passage there is one prerequisite for this teaching: the one who is teaching must first let the word of Christ richly dwell in him or her. What we must be teaching is not just our opinion but what we have gained through immersion in the word of Christ.

There is a place for passing on something learned from experience, but the real basis of our teaching must be the word of Christ. Jesus' last words in Matthew's Gospel contain the charge to teach others everything he had commanded. None of us will be prepared to teach another by filling ourselves up with the latest psychobabble on afternoon TV or self-help perspective from a popular magazine. We will be prepared to teach others by first being filled with the word of Christ. We may not be recognized as one of the "teachers" in the church who serve with elders and evangelists, but in another sense we are all teachers. It is to be part of what we do with one another. The two of us are recognized as teachers in our congregation, but we often find ourselves being taught by others who may even be young Christians.

Admonishing One Another

The second word used here, translated "admonish," is the Greek word *noutheteo*. This is not a bad translation if we understand what the English word means: (1) to caution, advise or counsel against something, (2) to reprove or scold, especially in a mild and goodwilled manner, and (3) to urge to a duty. *Noutheteo* means to warn or to counsel, always with the good of the other person in mind. To admonish is not to rebuke, although that may eventually be needed. It is used in Plato's writings to describe Socrates taking aside one of his students and carefully giving him cautionary counsel he believes will keep him from making certain mistakes.

Noutheteo is used frequently in the New Testament and describes a significant way Christians are to be involved with each other. Paul tells the Ephesian elders,

> Therefore be on the alert, remembering that night and day for a period of three years I did not cease to admonish each one with tears. (Acts 20:31, NASB)

He wrote to the Colossians,

> And we proclaim Him, admonishing every man and teaching every man with all wisdom, that we may present every man complete in Christ. (Colossians 1:28, NASB)

But Paul shows clearly in Romans that this practice is not just something for leaders:

> And concerning you, my brethren, I myself also am convinced that you yourselves are full of goodness, filled with all knowledge and able also to admonish one another. (Romans 15:14, NASB)

Illustrating the variety of input we are to give one another, Paul told the Thessalonians,

> And we urge you, brethren, admonish the unruly, encourage the fainthearted, help the weak, be patient with everyone. (1 Thessalonians 5:14, NASB)

When I (Tom) see the meanings of *noutheteo*, I think of another English word that we use more often than "admonish" and that is the word "coach"—one who trains or gives advice or instruction. It is not uncommon in our day to find people who are paying someone to be their "life coach." There is even an International Federation of Life Coaches. In the body of Christ we should have relationships with a number of people who can give us life coaching in a variety of areas. But just as important, we must realize that we can give other people coaching when we see the need for it.

Speaking the Truth in Love

This is probably a good time to introduce another text that does not use the word *noutheteo*, but certainly has the same idea.

To the Ephesians Paul wrote,

> Instead, speaking the truth in love, we will in all things grow up into him who is the Head, that is, Christ. (Ephesians 4:15)

This is really what admonishing or good coaching is: speaking the truth to someone but not harshly or with anything other than their good in mind. Paul says we need this practice in our relationships with one another in order that we may grow up—mature and develop—in Christ. In other words, this practice will help us to change, to be transformed.

To make this practical, let us look at some examples, realizing that almost any area of life can become a topic for such advice, counsel or warning. Perhaps you observe a brother who is not engaging in the fellowship, the common life. He seems to stay to himself. You may notice that someone is insensitive or self-focused. Maybe a sister seems dominated by negative and critical attitudes. In some cases you may see that someone overindulges in food or drink or something else. In other cases you may see someone who is too serious and unrelatable. In such a case, it is not that they have sinned. They just need some coaching in lightening up and having fun. One caution: you may not be the best person to talk with someone. (See question 1 in the section below for some guidance on this point.)

We may know of someone who is taking a job where he could be subject to some strong and new temptations. Knowing some of his weaknesses, it may be most needful for us to have a talk with him where we give some cautions and warnings. You are not making his decision for him. That remains for him.

From conversations with someone you may see that time spent in Bible study and prayer has been marginalized.

As we are writing this I (Tom) am seeing the need to talk with a man about his tendency to dominate group meetings and not encourage others or draw them out. By the time you read this, I will have had that conversation. You hopefully get the idea.

For those of us who want to become more like Christ, there is an almost endless list of things we can benefit from having input on. We do not give this input to stand in judgment on one another but to help one another be transformed. And any input that we give must be in response to and in concert with the conviction of the Spirit within us. (See appendix 2 for more thoughts about the Spirit's work in our relationships.)

SEVERAL QUESTIONS

1. Who can best admonish or coach someone?

A person with a close relationship is often in the best position, but in some cases, that person may not have as much credibility to address a certain area as someone else. It is crucial that whoever gives the input should himself or herself be a person with humility and one who demonstrates in his or her life a genuine desire for this kind of coaching and help. Remember where we started in this chapter: the number one credential is someone who is allowing the word of Christ to richly dwell in them.

2. What is the goal of this?

Maybe it would be good to first say what the goal is not. (1) It is not to make the person giving the admonishment look good or the person receiving it look bad. (2) It is not to gain a position of authority or superiority. (3) It is not to force someone to do something they do not want to do. (4) It is not to embarrass someone. (5) It is not to keep people in line. None of this would be true of a relationship conducted according to the grace of God.

The goal, quite simply, is to help another person grow and change and be transformed more fully into the image of Christ. Such growth will be for their benefit and for the benefit of those around them. It will strengthen the body of Christ.

3. How does teaching and admonishing bring growth?

First, it causes us who do it to examine ourselves more carefully. Ask some parents how much more carefully they watched their own lives when they started giving input to their children. "Do as I say, not as I do" is a most ineffective approach.

Second, it takes relationships much deeper. When we teach and admonish one another, we are getting down to some real issues, not just palling around. It lets people know we really care about them and are willing to even take some risks for them.

Finally, it really helps people give attention to important issues in their lives and see that there are others who want to help them make changes. When combined with other things we describe in this book, you see real changes in people's lives.

4. When can this work?

To answer this, let us first say that there is a corollary to this principle. If God intends for people to teach and admonish me, then that means he also intends for me to be grateful for those who do that and for me to receive what they are giving me. And there we have the answer.

This works and changes lives when we are eager to listen, to learn and to change. So every time we read in Scripture that we are to admonish one another, we must also see that is, at the same time, a call for us to be eager to receive such admonishment, coaching, advice and instruction.

The last time that I (Tom) taught on this subject I gave the class this assignment:
- Ask someone who knows you well this week: What do you perceive is my attitude toward being taught, admonished, counseled and corrected?
- Ask that same person: Is there anything in my life that you have thought about talking to me about but have held back for any reason or have not been sure how it would go if you did?

Before I taught the class, I accepted my own assignment. I asked a close brother, who is about the age of my oldest daughter, what he saw in me as regards my attitude toward being taught or corrected. He was encouraging. When I asked him the second question, he thought a minute and then told me that there were some things he needed to point out to me. As he responded to my request, amazingly or not-so-amazingly, I found some defensive feelings rising within me. But I settled in, listened and learned some things I needed to hear. Yes, hearing input can be tough, even when we have specifically asked for it, but it is so good for us.

We need our brothers and sisters. We need the kind of relationships in which we will speak the truth in love to one another. If there has been apathy, let it be replaced by love. If there has been fear, let it be replaced by faith. Avoid the extremes of brutal truth and insincere flattery. Speak the truth in love. By so doing, we will grow and change.

Making It Real

1. What are your own tendencies? Do you naturally like to give advice and correction, or do you shy away from that kind of interaction? What are the strengths and weaknesses of both tendencies?

2. What would you say to the person who responds to this chapter by saying, "I think we have to be really careful here. I just don't think we should be judging each other and throwing stones at one another."

3. What are some different ways you can speak the truth to someone? What will it mean to speak the truth in love? Give examples from your life when someone spoke the truth to you in the right way and how it changed you.

4. How and when do you have the most difficult time putting into practice this part of the "one another" life?

5. How can you see yourself beginning to do what is talked about in this chapter? What help or encouragement will you need?

6. What commitment do you want to make to your brothers and sisters about your desire to receive this kind of input and help?

7. How do you feel about accepting the class assignment described at the end of the chapter and doing it this week?

7
Confessing Sins to One Another

While the idea of teaching and admonishing others may frighten us, many of us freeze at the thought of confessing our sins to other people. We will often go through a variety of mental gymnastics to try and rationalize why we do not need to do it. We are often so adept at this avoidance that in the end we may convince ourselves that it is actually in the best interest of others that we not do it. In trying to avoid this need or practice, we are foolishly trying to escape something that is good, healthy and, most of all, in keeping with the whole message of the gospel. If you struggle with confessing your sins, this chapter might be the most liberating in the book.

Even if there were no specific calls for us to be a confessing people, the whole tenor of Scripture would lead us in that direction.

- The frequent emphasis on humility would bring us here.
- The teaching we will look at in the next chapter about bearing one another's burdens (of sin) is made so much more possible by openness and confession.
- The first of the Beatitudes, "Blessed are the poor in spirit" (Matthew 5:3), calls us to abandon all pretenses and be open about our need.
- The central message of discipleship, to deny ourselves and take up the cross, is dodged when we hide our sin and self-

ishly protect an identity that is not real.
- All of these can be summed up with the theme of chapter 2 of this book: to conduct our relationships, not according to worldly wisdom, but according to God's grace. The world's wisdom tells us to hide our sin; God's grace sets us free from the need for deception.

With such an understanding of how a Christ follower is to be, it is not surprising, then, that there are clear, straightforward statements about how confession is needed in our relationships. Consider first James 5:13–16 as found in the New American Standard Bible:

> Is any one of you in trouble? He should pray. Is anyone happy? Let him sing songs of praise. Is any one of you sick? He should call the elders of the church to pray over him and anoint him with oil in the name of the Lord. And the prayer offered in faith will make the sick person well; the Lord will raise him up. If he has sinned, he will be forgiven. Therefore confess your sins to each other and pray for each other so that you may be healed. The prayer of a righteous man is powerful and effective.

What is envisioned here is a community of believers. Within this fellowship one finds trouble, prayer, happiness, singing, sickness, more prayer, confession of sin and more prayer. Just as the sharing of sorrows and joys will be part of the fellowship, so, too, will be the confession of sin. All of this is what keeps it real, and the confession of sin is what takes us to a greater depth. It is a picture of people knowing and being known—no duplicity, no hiddenness, no fakery.

The end of verse 16 is frequently quoted: "The prayer of a

righteous man is powerful and effective." But according to Scripture, who is a righteous person? Is he not one who does not conceal sin but confesses it and renounces it (Proverbs 28:13)? Is he not one who confesses sin openly before others and says, "God, have mercy on me a sinner" (Luke 18:13)? Indeed is this not the one who goes home justified (made righteous) before God (Luke 18:14)? Isn't the person in James 5 who confesses his sins to another and asks others for their prayers, the one who himself can now pray powerfully and effectively?

Siamese Twins of Fellowship

Consider a second passage in 1 John:

> But if *we walk in the light,* as he is in the light, we have fellowship with one another, and the blood of Jesus, his Son, purifies us from all sin.
> If we claim to be without sin, we deceive ourselves and the truth is not in us. If *we confess our sins,* he is faithful and just and will forgive us our sins and purify us from all unrighteousness. If we claim we have not sinned, we make him out to be a liar and his word has no place in our lives.
> (1 John 1:7–10, emphasis added)

As mentioned in chapter one, I (Tom) read thirty years ago the suggestion that we should think of verse 7 and verse 9 as the Siamese twins of 1 John. In verse 7 to "walk in the light" is to bring your life out in the open, to hide nothing in the folds of your cloak. Such an openness brings purification by the blood of Jesus. Again, those who are not hiding anything are made righteous.

In verse 9 we have the same idea with different words. If we "confess our sins" we are purified from all unrighteousness.

Walking in the light and confessing sins mean the same thing, and so both lead to the same result—being made righteous. So not only are verse 7 and verse 9 parallel, they are also parallel to James 5:16. This is interesting in view of how, otherwise, these two letters are dramatically different in style and approach.

But notice something important in verse 7: this living in the light with one another leads to fellowship (*koinonia*) with one another. In other words, doing God's will in your relationships takes those relationships even deeper. Haven't you seen it happen?

My wife (Tom writing here) recently came home from a time with a small group of women. At dinner she had shared with them some things she had recently learned about herself. She walked in the light with them, that is, she confessed her sin. You probably do not have to guess the result. They had heart-level fellowship with one another as others were also open. She came home with somewhat of a glow.

Long before that evening she had taken seriously God's call for her to build relationships with these Christians. But once in these relationships, she practiced the transparency we are discussing. She had to humble herself (and die to herself) to do it, but she lived out the baptized life and God gave resurrection.

I always feel a bit sorry for people who try to argue that we do not have to confess to one another—just to God or just to a priest behind a partition. I feel sorry for them because they are running from something that could give them greater freedom and allow them to enjoy deeper fellowship. Most "spiritually" or "Christianly" minded people believe in some kind of confession, but if the confession you employ does not bring about greater fellowship (*koinonia*) and transformation, could it possibly not be what we find here in 1 John?

Vital Lessons

Looking at the two passages from James and 1 John together, let us think about some lessons that can be learned:

1. Sin is still a reality—even in Christ. We all know this from experience, but we also see it clearly affirmed in Scripture. This is a book about transformational relationships, not perfect relationships. Many of us can look at ways God has used a relationship to transform us and mold us, even though there was sin in that relationship, and mistakes and disappointments and failures, at times. Everyone who seeks to be involved in the relationships we are describing here will find themselves on both sides of such things—sinning and being sinned against.

2. Christ has freed us to be real. We admitted our lostness. We have been born into God's family. We are his. We were baptized into the name of the Father, the name of the Son and the name of the Holy Spirit. That is our identity. We wear God's name. We no longer have to prove anything. We no longer have to pretend or conceal. We may struggle with walking in the light particularly about some things, but the love of Christ compels us and reminds us and reassures us.

3. We should not be shocked or disillusioned when someone confesses. Having said that, I know that there will be times when we are caught off guard. Maybe we have assumed that a certain person would never do this or that, and it comes like a kick in the stomach when we hear certain confessions. But if we are to have a fellowship where people feel encouraged to walk in the light, we must all seek not to react when we find that one of our fellow sinners has sinned.

A "stunning" confession becomes a moment of truth for us. Will we look down on others the way the unjustified and unrighteous Pharisee did in Jesus' parable (Luke 18)? Will we in that moment reveal that we are more unrighteous than the person who has just confessed to us—but not nearly as humble about admitting it? Or will we see that we all are capable of bad things and in need of grace?

4. The sooner we can walk in the light, the better. When something is right to do—sooner rather than later is almost always the best advice. The longer something stays concealed, the more the demons of the darkness have time to work.

While we were working on this book, I was on the phone with Steve about a matter unrelated to the book. He said something that irritated me (not a normal thing for him to do, by the way). I responded in a most edgy way to his inquiry. A few more awkward sentences were exchanged, and then I said I wanted to go back to my reaction and to ask his forgiveness. He freely gave it.

What would have happened if I had waited? I could have put it off again and again as it became harder to bring up. Eventually, I might have forgotten about it—but something in me and in our relationship would not have been healed. Our fellowship would have suffered.

At this point let me say that far too many brothers in Christ who are caught in a trap and cycle of lust and pornography suffer greatly because they do not quickly walk in the light. If this is your situation, get with someone who will really help you, and bring it all into the light.

SEVERAL QUESTIONS

Usually this subject of confession brings up quite a list of questions. Let us look at a few:

1. **Neither James nor John mentions repentance. What if repentance is not in a person's heart?**

We see three things to say about this:
   (a) Confession is never done from humility if it does not involve repentance. A person may act sorry, but without repentance, which shows humility toward God and toward others, it is worldly sorrow. There are religious traditions that have reinforced the idea that confession itself is valuable, but one does not have to come from one of those traditions to think this way. I have known people who seem to feel more spiritual if they are confessing, while at the same time they are showing no fruit of repentance. They deceive only themselves. Confession without repentance is in the same file with faith without action—it is useless.

   (b) Confession is self-focused and not God-focused if it does not seek to please him. Without repentance, confession is being done for some self-serving reason (e.g., to gain sympathy, to appear open, to avoid a charge of hypocrisy). It is not being done out of passion for God and response to the cross.

   (c) Confession of sin must involve forsaking that sin. This is stated plainly in Proverbs 28:13 (NASB): "He who conceals his transgressions will not prosper, but he who confesses and forsakes them will find compassion." The opposite of concealing sin is confessing and forsaking those sins. James and John would have concurred with Paul in their understanding of repentance as Jesus taught them all.

In our relationships with one another, hearing someone's confession should be seen as step one. Helping them form a plan of "forsaking" is step two. Especially with long-standing patterns of sin, we may be just enabling another person if we do not ask questions and help them think through a plan of action. Praying with them would be step three, and following up with encouragement would be step four.

2. What is the power of confession?

In some ways the answer here is a review of things we have already noted. But do not skip this. We have a few new wrinkles.

(a) Confession is powerful because it brings the forgiveness of sin and purifies us from all unrighteousness (1 John 1:7, 9). Opening our lives to the light of God brings a cleansing power. The Greek verb is in the present (continuous) tense, i.e., his blood keeps on cleansing us (think of the continuous action of windshield wipers removing the falling rain and you have the picture). These verses speak of forgiveness and cleansing. God is doing more than forgiving; he is transforming us. That work of transformation is often carried on by our relationships. Once we have humbled ourselves before another and let someone know the real us, the door is open for us to be encouraged through that relationship to make changes.

(b) Confession brings fellowship with God and with brothers and sisters (again, 1 John 1:7–9). Some commentators insist that this is only a reference to fellowship with God, but with the way the term "one another" (*allelon*) is used throughout the New Testament and five more times in 1 John for Christian relationships, that is a hard case to make. Confession is not just good for the soul, it is good for the souls that are seeking unity and partnership.

(c) To look at something not yet mentioned: confession represents a strong stand against Satan. In John 8:44 Jesus described Satan as "a liar and the father of lies." "Resist the devil and he will flee from you," says James (4:7). We are never more in his grasp than when we deceive or conceal. We are never more immune to his schemes than when we are living transparently in the light.

(d) Finally, we would mention the contagiousness of confession. Scripture speaks often of the power of example. One person's example in confession can encourage the openness of others, and often that is the beginning of widespread revival and times of transformation.

3. Can confession in the church ever be turned in the wrong way so that harm is the result?

It is hard to think of a biblical subject that cannot be misused. This is true of grace, discipleship, baptism, the Lord's Supper, election and advice. The list is long. But it is good to note how confession can be used or handled hurtfully. We think rather quickly of five possibilities:

(a) If we react with condemnation—How devastating it can be for someone to get the courage to be open, only to hear the other person say, "I can't believe you did (or thought) that!" or "You don't know hard that is to hear." Even if we feel that kick in the stomach we referred to earlier, it is time for us to focus on the other person, not our own sense of injury or hurt.

(b) If we gossip and do not keep confidences—All we have to do here is apply the Golden Rule, i.e., handle someone else's confession the way we would want ours handled.

We may give advice to the person about who we think they should confess to, but it is not our prerogative to pass on their information without their permission.

(c) If we use it to label people or to control people—We know of situations where someone confessed being prideful, for example, and then the person hearing the confession never allowed them out of that box. It was brought up later as a kind of club to beat them with or manipulate them. Yes, in our coaching of one another we may have to come back to something that was confessed and ask, "Is this an example of what you shared earlier?" But we must be careful to communicate hope and how we believe God can cleanse and transform.

(d) If we think it is our role to "fix them"—In relationships where there is confession, we have responsibility. But we must watch out for what a friend of mine calls "overresponsibility." Now that you have shared your sin with me, you still have the main responsibility to deal with it. I should pray for you, encourage you and ask helpful questions of you, but it is not my responsibility to fix you. Whenever someone feels this way, a very unhealthy dynamic is likely to develop that hurts both people.

(e) If leaders do not do it, but expect others to do it—Or to put it a slightly different way: when confession only goes one way in a relationship. Such hierarchical confession accentuates everything bad about hierarchical relationships. Some of us can say that we have "been there and done that" and do not want to go there again. Any religious system that is set up to promote one-way confession is bound to become dysfunctional and unhealthy.

3. Is confession risky?

In so many situations, even when it involves those we feel the most safe with, we have to say, "absolutely." It is risky. But, so are many things we are called to do as disciples. This life of following Jesus is the righteous road, not the safe road. We did not misunderstand that, did we? In the process of doing the right thing in so many areas, we may get hurt, but did not Jesus pronounce blessings on those who suffer for righteousness' sake (Matthew 5:10)?

Most of the time in a healthy fellowship, confession will bring healthy results, but even when something gets twisted, it is still the right thing and will ultimately be blessed by God.

4. Is confession a painful thing or a joyful thing?

Yes!

5. How do we grow in this area?

(a) We would suggest that you start by being open even at the temptation level. If we learn to walk in the light about our temptations, we will accomplish two things: (1) we will get used to talking about life at that level, and (2) we will nip many things in the bud before they ever progress to sin.

(b) We have observed that one of the ways people grow in many areas is by first doing what we might call "overcorrecting." When I (Tom) was in college, my tennis coach taught me this principle. I was routinely hitting my first serve right on the tape at the top of the net. Knowing I was just missing some possible aces by inches, I tried to make a micro adjustment, but I continued to hit the tape. My coach urged me to overcorrect. He advised me to aim at least a foot above the net. Of course, as I did that I hit the ball beyond the service line. However, after doing that for a while, I was able to adjust the trajectory down some and then get some of those aces I needed. It would not hurt most of us to "overcorrect" for a while. If confession has not been part of the tenor of your life, try going a bit overboard with it. And then see if you are not able to find a good balance.

(c) Ask your spouse, roommate or close friend, "Do you find me to be a confessing person?" and "Would I be someone you would feel good about confessing to?" Then discuss the responses.

As with everything else in this book, we must be convinced that confession of sin is God's will, or it will not be something consistently in our lives. It rarely comes naturally. It is a decision made out of faith. The old saying is "Confession is good for the soul." Scripture supports that, but goes further. Confession is great for our relationships.

Making It Real

1. What have been your experiences of confessing your sins?
2. If there have been sinful responses, how do you need to process those?
3. How have you handled the confession of others? In what ways do you need to respond more righteously and helpfully?
4. How would you categorize yourself:
   - Seldom confess sin
   - Confess only when there is "big" sin
   - Consistently confess sin
   - Am open even about temptations
5. Why do you think you are the way you are? Are there changes you want to make?
6. How does confession fit with the way of the cross?

Bearing One Another's Burdens

> Brethren, even if anyone is caught in any trespass, you who are spiritual, restore such a one in a spirit of gentleness; each one looking to yourself, so that you too will not be tempted. Bear one another's burdens, and thereby fulfill the law of Christ.
>
> Galatians 6:1–2, NASB

While we see most people still living with self on the throne, we do see a good number of people who help each other with things in life that are difficult. We (the Joneses) recently saw an episode of the TV show "Extreme Makeover: Home Edition." It caught our attention because we knew quite well the Massachusetts town that was featured in the story. Hundreds of residents wrote the TV network urging them to rebuild a home for a family after a husband and father of three had been severely disabled in an accident. When the network picked them for the makeover, the town poured out to help with the project.

Even as this is being written, aid is pouring in from around the world for two catastrophes in Asia that have taken in excess of 100,000 lives and left millions homeless.

So when Paul wrote to the churches of Galatia and told them they should bear one another's burdens, was he saying that Christians should at least do what so many people in the world, who are not believers, do rather instinctively? Or did he have more in mind?

Consider the Context

As we pointed out in chapter 1 the context of the passage is very important. In the verses preceding Galatians 6:1-2, Paul has spoken of our choice to live according to the sinful nature or according to the Spirit. Chapter 5 ends with a call to stop sins that destroy relationships. The first verse of chapter 6 describes what we do when sin persists in someone's life. Those who are spiritually-minded and concerned about others and the church must get involved. Their goal must be to restore their brother or sister—that is, bring them back into line with God's plan for righteousness.

In this context Paul says we must "bear one another's burdens." While there is plenty of teaching in the Scriptures that would call us to care for each other and be there for each other when fire or illness or tragedy happens, that does not seem to be the first thing on Paul's mind here. No, the burden that we must first think about is the burden produced by sin.

We are to get so deeply involved in helping our friend overcome his sin, that we will actually be exposing ourselves to some dangerous temptation. As we help him, we must be careful that we do not get pulled into his sin. If his sin is being conceited and provoking and envying others (Galatians 5:26), he will almost certainly have a bitter spirit that could defile us (Hebrews 12:15). If his sin is lust, as we endeavor to help him, we will undoubtedly be reminded of things that we ourselves have to guard against.

But while we watch ourselves and guard our own hearts, we must help him deal with the burden that sin puts on him and on the church. In this context Paul says, "Carry each other's burdens, and in this way you will fulfill the law of Christ" (v2). What a remarkable attitude and commitment we are called to have.

Here is William or Wanda who has been seen by us to be in sin. It is their own doing, not ours. They have created the problems, not us. And yet the spirit of Jesus calls us to treat their sin as if it were our own and help them bear that burden all the way out of their life. We cannot repent for them, but we can exhort and encourage and pray with them.

The Principle of Christ

Now notice a crucial phrase: in doing this we will fulfill the law of Christ. You could look at this and say Jesus gave us a command to love one another, and so that is one of the laws of Christ. If we help our friend we will be obeying the command. I suspect Paul means something much deeper.

The word "law" is used in the New Testament the way we often use it. We talk about the law of gravity. By this we mean the principle of gravity. We talk about the law of the harvest—you reap what you sow (referred to by Paul just five verses down). This refers to a principle. It is not so much a command to be obeyed.

The law of Christ, then, very likely refers to the principle we see at work in Christ—the principle of being willing to bear the sins of others and find God's power in doing this. Isaiah 53:4-5 describes the work of the Suffering Servant.

> Surely he took up our infirmities
>   and carried our sorrows,
> yet we considered him stricken by God,
>   smitten by him, and afflicted.
> But he was pierced for our transgressions,

> he was crushed for our iniquities;
> the punishment that brought us peace was upon him,
> and by his wounds we are healed.

Isaiah describes a messiah who will take up and carry our infirmities and sorrows, no doubt often caused by our transgression and iniquities, even though he had nothing to do with them. He would take them up and bear them so fully that the punishment and wounds that are the consequences of those sins would all be put on him.

In the New Testament Peter alludes to Isaiah's text when he speaks of Jesus this way:

> He himself bore our sins in his body on the tree, so that we might die to sins and live for righteousness; by his wounds you have been healed. (1 Peter 2:24)

Jesus does not just call us to see our sin and repent of it. He took it on himself and he bore it, and he carried it out to Golgotha's hill where it could be crucified. When we come to Christ in faith and baptism, we accept that crucifixion and make it our own, dying to sin.

And now we are called to follow in his steps. He did not self-righteously say, "That is not my sin. It is yours." And neither must we. We may be wearied or discouraged or even angry because of our brother's sin, but to follow Jesus we must care enough to help him overcome it. Will that cost us something? You bet it will. Time, effort, emotional pain and probably some physical distress, to name just four things. But it cost Jesus all that to bear our burden.

And so when we get involved in someone's life to help them move—not a piano or a refrigerator or financial challenge—but sin, and to move it out to the place of the cross, we are fulfilling the law of Christ, the very principle of Jesus. We are showing him to the world.

SEVERAL QUESTIONS

As we look at this it would seem we need to ask and answer several questions:

1. How is the bearing of someone's sin to be done?

Maybe we should first say how it is not to be done. It should not be done rashly and impulsively. It should not be done like the irritated parent who finally has all he or she can take from their child and lashes out at them. (Of course, that is not good for parents or children either.) While there are some things we should not do, there are a number of things that we ought to do.

(a) The action should be done with prayer. Paul says, "You who are spiritual…" To venture into the life of another person should never be done out of our confidence, even when we think we see clearly that someone has been overcome with something. In every such situation, we need the greatest of wisdom, and that should be something for which we pray (James 1:5).

(b) Listen and understand as fully as possible to what has happened. Ask questions. Get all the facts. Find out the background—where their emotions are and what is going on in their heart. Remember Proverbs 18:13: "He who answers before listening—that is his folly and his shame." Far too many of us want to give advice or correction before we have listened. This is a disturbing tendency because when we do this, we fail to connect emotionally with the person we want to help. And we often give responses that do not really meet the need.

(c) Relate to them. Where you can, share how you may have been tempted or have sinned in similar ways. Paul tells us that this whole process is to be done "gently." This was the term a Greek surgeon used to describe how a broken bone needed to be realigned. As you relate to a person, they will not feel that you are coming to self-righteously condemn them, but to truly help them bear their burden. You may need to give sober warnings, but those are much more likely to be heard if you have first done your best to relate to someone.

(d) Point to Scripture. It is Scripture that ultimately needs to train and correct—not you (2 Timothy 3:17). Show the person God's standard, how this sin is not a part of the new age of the kingdom, and help them understand that this is not a disagreement over taste and preference.

(e) Help them evaluate their heart. Is there a godly sorrow (Matthew 5: 4; 2 Corinthians 7:8–11)? If there is not, you are not ready to move on.

(f) Ask them what they see is needed to demonstrate repentance. Help them if they do not seem to see how far they need to go. Help them develop a plan of repentance.

(g) Take them all the way to the cross. Help them understand that until they take that sin to the place where it dies, they will not be set free.

(h) Assure them of your support and then give it. Follow up with encouragement and prayer. This is where the real test of "bearing their burden" comes and too often where we fail. Too often someone brings correction to another person, but then no one is there to help them with the follow-up that is so critical.

2. **When is helping each other in this way most likely not to happen?**

It is so important that we develop a culture in the church where what we read here is encouraged. It may never be easy, but we can grow a church culture where it is expected and the ground is prepared for it. But when is it most likely not to happen? There are two main answers:

(a) When relationships are superficial. Nothing we are talking about in this book is going to happen when people are content with shallow relationships. If people are not involved in each other's lives in a deeper and consistent basis, they are not going to even know when someone has strayed into sin, at least until something ugly and public emerges.

(b) When we feel our own burdens are quite enough and that we do not really need anybody else's. It is not hard for anybody to feel that. Most people I know have a lot on their plate. The daily demands of life, job, marriage, family and the weight of our own sin can seem all we can possibly handle. But if we give in to that thinking, we are missing something vital.

3. **When will this type of interaction happen in our relationships?**

(a) When relationships are real, open and deep. When we hardly know someone, it is a great challenge to put their issues on our radar screen, although there are times we must do that. However, when we know people and walk with them and feel with them and pray with them, we will know when they start leaving the path. And then if we see them drift into sin, we become bothered or distressed. We care about them and do not want to see them falling into the mire.

(b) When we feel our own burdens, but live with a servant heart, trusting God blesses those who care for others. In Philippians 2:4–5 Paul writes: "Each of you should look not only to your own interests, but also to the interests of others. Your attitude should be the same as that of Christ Jesus...." The whole life as a Christ follower is one of walking with the faith that he who loses his life will find it. Jesus demonstrated this truth in his death and resurrection, as Paul highlights in the verses that follow 4 and 5.

(c) When we understand that we are responsible for one another and accept that responsibility. Each of us should be grateful to be in a fellowship where others feel responsible for us. Woeful be the person who is prideful enough to think he can be what he should be on his own. Gratitude should lead us all to take responsibility for one another.

4. What is the corollary to this message?

As described earlier, often in Scripture there is a corollary that is just as true and is as much God's will as the teaching itself. In this case, if the Scripture tells you to restore me and bear my burden, the corollary is that God wants me to allow you to do that. God always wants his word to bear fruit. If I am not humble and willing to allow you in my life to help me change and to help me carry that sin out to the place of the cross, God's plan is not fulfilled.

The teaching of Galatians 6:2 is that we must bear the burdens of others. The corollary is that we must allow other people to do that in our lives, or more than that, welcome it and be thankful for it. The corollary is that any spirit of pride and independence must be overcome as is evident in every chapter of this book. We must admit that we need help and be grateful for God's plan to bring it to us.

How much do we want sin to be carried out of our lives and crucified? How about in the lives of others? How crucial do we believe this to be? What sacrifices are we willing to make?

5. **Finally, is there a principle here that applies to other issues besides the burden of sin?**

Absolutely. We can all see through an attitude says, "Sister, I want to help you with sin in your life, but maybe you could find someone else to help you get through this cancer treatment." If we are willing to help each other with the most serious thing in our lives—the sin that affects our relationship with God and other people—then surely we will be willing to help with those things that even worldly friends are concerned about.

Jesus cares about all our cares, worries and anxieties (1 Peter 5:7). He wants to help us with them all. In the body we are to mourn with those who mourn (Romans 12:15). If one part suffers, every part is to suffer with him or her (1 Corinthians 12:26). A friend and dear brother of ours is in serious kidney failure at age thirty-nine. Dozens in the fellowship have rallied around him and his family. That is as it should be. Right here in Galatians 6 Paul makes our responsibility clear when he writes: "Therefore, as we have opportunity, let us do good to all people, especially to those who belong to the family of believers" (v10).

In dealing with any burden, Ecclesiastes 4:9 is true: "Two are better than one, because they have a good return for their work." This is true if the burden is sin. It is true if it is working through grief. We really do need one another. Your brother's burden—any burden—is your burden. And as the whole body is functioning in a healthy way, there will be people close in with anyone who needs help with their burden. Bearing the burdens of others has a long history among loving families, many churches and tightly-knit communities. However, it has been far too rare to find spiritual communities where this is understood in context and put into practice. When it is done, we often save a soul from death (James 5:20) and help one back on to the road to transformation.

Making It Real

1. What burdens do you find it easiest to help others with?
2. How do you feel about getting out of your comfort zone in relationships?
3. How do you feel about initiating with someone, the way Galatians 6:1 describes it, when you see that they are getting trapped in a sin? When is the last time you did this?
4. This week, who are you aware of that is struggling with some burden (sin, temptation or otherwise)? What steps can you take to share their load?
5. How have you communicated to others that you want their help in bearing your burdens—especially the burden of sin?
6. How does this concept fit with the way of the cross?

Encouraging One Another

We all need more encouragement. Right? Some days more than others. Recently, I (Steve) was struggling to write a chapter for this book. Call it "writer's block" or whatever, but I was not getting very far very fast. So I call my friend Tom Jones—co-conspirator in the teaching of lessons and now the writing of a book on the subject. I was stuck. He offered a "word of encouragement" about the finished product. "Don't overthink it. Just write and we'll work with that." Wow! Simple. Of course he shared a few brief stories of his own and other similar experiences. It helped. It worked. I was encouraged. I started writing.

Other days the problem may be more serious. A health challenge. A death in the family. Losing a job. Whatever it may be—we all need encouragement. We probably need it a whole lot more than we think or expect. Wait a minute. We definitely need it much more than we think. Kind of like water. We drink when we are thirsty, right? Well, after two kidney stones last summer, the doctor convinced me that I need to drink more, much more, like twice as much as I thought I needed if I wanted to keep from having more excruciatingly painful encounters with little barbed rocks.

So it is with encouragement. We vastly underestimate our deep-seated need to be encouraged, to be inspired, to be lifted out of the rut of mundane, ordinary existence to see the real spiritual significance of the things we do every day. I (Steve) was struck recently by a line in a Louis L'Amour western. (I must admit—I am a lifelong fan of Zane Grey and Louis L'Amour.) The protagonist said upon being referred to as a hero:

> "It is an empty word out here, ma'am. It is a word for writers and sitters by the fire. Out here a man does what the situation demands. Out on the frontier we do not have heroes, only people doing what is necessary at the time."[1]

We need to see the heroic in the day-to-day things we do: making that call, writing that note, sharing the good news in a chance encounter, taking the time to be a friend. Do you get the idea? We get so bogged down with life in this physical world that we fail to see and enjoy the eternal significance of the little opportunities that God puts in our way every day. We need others to help us see. To give us perspective. To encourage us.

Parakaleois

There are four key passages that enjoin us to encourage one another, but before we look at them we need to spend a little time on the meaning of the Greek word for "encourage." *Parakaleo* is the word behind the NIV's translation of "encourage." It is used much more widely in the New Testament than in the four passages I will mention, so we need to get more insight into the wealth and depth of emotion that it connotes.

Parakaleo is used twenty-eight times in the Gospels and Acts, most frequently in the sense of "to beg" or "plead" but also may be used as "to comfort." In Acts as the writing progresses, it is more often translated "encourage." In the letters *parakaleo* is usually an emotional appeal—translated with "plead," "appeal" or, most frequently, "urge." Seventeen times it is translated "encourage."

---

1. Louis L'Amour, *The Lonesome Gods* (New York: Bantam Books, 1984), 24.

The command form, usually translated "I urge you," occurs often in the letters in the portions that mark the end of the first part of the letter and the beginning of the second, generally more practical, part. The English translation seems to depend upon who is addressed and the desired outcome. For example, a parent asking for healing for a sick child is said to "beg" or "plead" while a leader addressing a group of new disciples is said to "encourage." My favorite Greek lexicon (Bauer-Arndt-Gingrich) puts it like this:

1. To call to one's side (literally); to summon. (I like the first, don't you? Kind of a "Come on; we can do this!" attitude.)
2. Appeal to, urge, exhort, encourage.
3. Entreat, implore, comfort and cheer up.

Do not forget as well the etymology of our English word from the old French *encoragier*—"to put courage in." That is cool. We definitely can use some extra courage.

FOUR KEY PASSAGES

So with this understanding of the word *parakaleo* in mind, let us look at what these biblical texts have in store for us:

1 Thessalonians 4:18

Therefore encourage each other with these words.

The first thing we see is there should be content to our encouragement. In this context Paul is specifically talking about using his words about the Second Coming of Jesus as the content to encourage the brothers and sisters, to help them to live their lives with the fact and nature of Jesus' return in mind.

The point is that our encouragement is to be more than a pat on the back. Our words need an emotional appeal based on specific biblical content. A few years back, as I (still Steve) was wrestling with the devastating incursion of multiple sclerosis into my life which left me paralyzed on the left side, a rather challenging opportunity to serve the church presented itself. In my humanistic thinking all I could see were impossible obstacles. A brother challenged me to stop thinking about what I could not do and to have faith in what God could do. I do not remember the details, but it was not a fun conversation.

His encouragement led Diane and me into a great time in the ministry and the development of some lifelong friends. Although the obstacles were many, I look back on that time with much fondness. Without a brother's encouragement to have more faith in God in this situation, my whole perspective on what I am able to do today, with God's help, might have been seriously crippled.

1 Thessalonians 5:11

> Therefore encourage one another and build each other up, just as in fact you are doing.

Encouragement should move us toward maturity. Encouragement is often combined with strengthening (Acts 14:22, 15:32; 1 Thessalonians 3:2; 2 Thessalonians 2:17) or with the idea of "building up" or "edification."

Again we are not talking about just being nice. Not just a "How are you? Fine." dialogue, but something that fits into a pattern of life that helps us move along a path toward spiritual maturity. We need growth in our relationship with God, in our interactions in the body, in our purity, in our discipline, in our prayer life, in our knowledge of the Word, in our outreach, in our character. Are you getting the idea that we all have a lot of growing to do? And we all need plenty of encouragement applied in liberal doses to do it.

Are you growing? The longer we are around, the more important this becomes. Yes, baby Christians need loads of instruction and encouragement, but so do the rest of us. The danger many of us face is a spiritual midlife crisis. We get stuck. We stop growing, learning and changing. The pressures of life increase. Dreams die or get crowded out by the day-to-day routine. You wake up one Sunday, and you don't have any clue why you should get up and go to church, except "that is just what we do."

We have to keep growing, learning, challenging ourselves to take a step out of the ordinary. Go for a prayer walk or stay up all night to pray. Fast (maybe it has been awhile). Go on a personal spiritual retreat. Sign up for a mission trip. Take your family vacation visiting the church in a third world country. Open your heart up to disciples who can help you. Do something that will get you out of your routine.

But do not stop here. Look around you and see others who are still stuck, and realize how uniquely qualified you are to encourage them to get the wheels turning again. Some day, years from now, they may recall a life-altering conversation with you.

Hebrews 3:12–13

> See to it, brothers, that none of you has a sinful, unbelieving heart that turns away from the living God. But encourage one another daily, as long as it is called Today, so that none of you may be hardened by sin's deceitfulness.

For me (Steve) this has long been a favorite passage. I guess the idea of daily encouragement resonated with me. It seemed to

fit in with my idea of what the early church was like. Not a once-a-week thing, but real involvement in each other's lives.
We underestimate the power and deceitfulness of our sin. We fail to realize the strength of discouragement and its ability to gradually eat away at our conviction and our faith. We need each other. We need that daily encouragement to keep us sharp, on our toes and ready to fight the battle, to stay faithful to the end.
There is a strong sense of spiritual obligation in this text. "See to it." Not "hope that it happens" or "someone will surely do it." See to it. Make sure it happens. Who? You. You are a Christian, are you not? A disciple of Jesus? Then this applies. Personally.
Encourage daily? Is that really practical? I mean we are so busy these days. Do I have to tell you how busy I am? Yes, we are busy. Our lives get crowded with ever increasing "stuff" to do. Okay, so we are busy, but we also have more ways to stay in touch than ever before. The ubiquitous cell phone. ("Can you hear me now?") E-mail. Instant Messenger. Texting. Facebook. There is no excuse.
I remember just a few years ago (about twenty now…time flies), when we (Steve and Diane) were living in Buenos Aires, Argentina. For six months our phone did not work. None of the phones in the neighborhood worked. (Pre-cell phone days—can you imagine?) The nearest phone, a pay phone in a café, was two blocks away. So our ministry had to become very creative. Our house became a revolving door. Brothers would drop by after work or before work. Meals almost always involved somebody from church who more often than not had just dropped in. Messages were passed by word of mouth. Every trip out usually involved dropping by to see someone or at least making a few

quick telephone calls. You know, it was great. We learned to make it work, even on a daily basis. We can do this. Encourage each other daily.

Hebrews 10:25

> Let us not give up meeting together, as some are in the habit of doing, but let us encourage one another—and all the more as you see the Day approaching.

A brother here in Nashville opened my eyes to something I had never seen in this passage. I had always focused on the meeting together as a reference to the public assembly (and with a form of the Greek *sunagogue* being used here, that likely was the first meaning). However, throughout his internship and residency to become a medical doctor, he had been forced to miss services of the church. He latched on to the idea that meeting together did not have to refer exclusively to the services of the church, but that it also applies to our getting together as brothers at any time, whether over lunch, breakfast, coffee or in a prayer walk. He took it as a call to meet with his brothers whenever he could make it happen. This understanding fits in with what we just saw in Hebrews 3 and the "daily encouragement."

Obviously this point is not an excuse to miss the meetings of the church, but an added emphasis on the importance of our relationships outside of these regular meetings. We think that as Christians many of us take the injunction here too lightly. With all the youth sports, job demands and school activities, there seems to be a growing acceptance of not getting together, of letting other things crowd out meeting together. It is particularly refreshing in this environment to see that an Atlanta-based company, CHICK-FIL-A, continues to stay closed on Sundays so their employees can go to church and be with their families. Maybe we need to reexamine our convictions.

At any rate, the major point here is not just to show up at the meetings of the church. We need to have a consistent pattern of getting with brothers and sisters to encourage and to be encouraged.

Let Us Do It!

Hopefully what we have written here convinces us of our great need for encouragement, and the need to give it. What should be clear as well is the command form of these scriptural instructions:

> *Encourage each other with these words.*
> *Encourage one another and build each other up.*
> *Encourage one another daily.*
> *Let us encourage one another.*

We are supposed to do this. God says it needs to be done. It is not an "optional accessory" to our late model Christianity. It is the very lifeblood of who we are as followers of Jesus.

Do it. You. Me.

Let's encourage one another.

Making It Real

1. How do you see your own need for encouragement?
2. What are you doing to ensure that you continue to grow as a disciple? Who is helping you? Who are you helping?
3. What can you do to give encouragement that has meaningful content and encouragement that moves people toward maturity?
4. How do you feel about this assignment: Go to one person in your family and one close Christian in the church (same gender as you) and ask: "What input can you give me about being more encouraging?"
5. What are your personal convictions about missing meetings of the body? What are they based on? Why does it matter?

10

Spurring One Another On

We come now to an expression that is rich in meaning, yet difficult to comprehend. We come to a command that may inspire us or frighten us: "spurring one another on." What does it mean, and what does it not mean? The answers to both of these questions are vital in importance.

The text of Hebrews 10:24–25 reads in the NIV:

> And let us consider how we may spur one another on toward love and good deeds. Let us not give up meeting together, as some are in the habit of doing, but let us encourage one another—and all the more as you see the Day approaching.

Back in chapter 6 when we looked at teaching and admonishing one another, we addressed some issues related to the ones we find here. We mentioned that some of us may be decidedly uncomfortable with this level of involvement, and we would never dream of "sticking our noses into someone else's business." On the other hand, others of us may have no second thoughts about asking others about very personal things and telling them exactly what we think they should do and expecting them to do it. Both of these can be unfaithful extremes. With this in mind let us turn to a deeper analysis of the text.

Consider the Context

In order to properly comprehend verses 24–25 and, even more importantly, to figure out how to use them, we need to look to the context for guidance. Let us look at the verses immediately preceding our text in the Holman CSB to give a fresh perspective:

> Therefore, brothers, since we have boldness to enter the sanctuary through the blood of Jesus, by the new and living way that He has inaugurated for us, through the curtain (that is, His flesh); and since we have a great high priest over the house of God, let us draw near with a true heart in full assurance of faith, our hearts sprinkled [clean] from an evil conscience and our bodies washed in pure water. Let us hold on to the confession of our hope without wavering, for He who promised is faithful. And let us be concerned about one another in order to promote love and good works, not staying away from our meetings, as some habitually do, but encouraging each other, and all the more as you see the day drawing near. (Hebrews 10:19–25)

Did you notice all the great spiritual blessings that we have, based on our relationship with Jesus?

- We have access to the Father through the blood and body of Jesus.
- We have a great high priest, guaranteeing closeness to God.
- We have full assurance. No doubts! Faith has an answer to every doubt.
- We have a clean heart and a clean conscience (maybe a cleansed conscience would be another way to put it).

- We have hope. Amen to that! What more can you say?
- We have a faithful God. He will not let us down. He will come through for us. He will be there when we most need him.

Then we come to our text, and we see that the author's focus on the tremendous benefits we have as a result of our relationship together in Christ calls us not to take lightly this fellowship we share, but to pursue it with greater vigor.

The context following verses 19–25 is also of great importance. Again we use the Holman CSB:

> And let us be concerned about one another in order to promote love and good works, not staying away from our meetings, as some habitually do, but encouraging each other, and all the more as you see the day drawing near.
> For if we deliberately sin after receiving the knowledge of the truth, there no longer remains a sacrifice for sins, but a terrifying expectation of judgment, and the fury of a fire about to consume the adversaries. If anyone disregards Moses' law, he dies without mercy, based on the testimony of two or three witnesses. How much worse punishment, do you think one will deserve who has trampled on the Son of God, regarded as profane the blood of the covenant by which he was sanctified, and insulted the Spirit of grace? For we know the One who has said, Vengeance belongs to Me, I will repay, and again, The Lord will judge His people. It is a terrifying thing to fall into the hands of the living God! (Hebrews 10:24–31)

"Terrifying" is the word used by the Hebrew writer. He obviously missed the courses Sensitivity 101 and Basic Political

Correctness 204 at the Galilean Apostolic Seminary. We have to acknowledge that we are not accustomed to talk like this, but we also have to remember that the standard is the Scriptures and not our present day experiences or our cultural environment. The major thing that strikes us is the seriousness of this whole matter. While we are confident of our access to the Father through the blood of Jesus and know that he has cleansed our consciences, we are still talking about some real shaking in your boots. Those made righteous will still be in awe of God (Revelation 1:17). God is not one to trifle with, and thus our involvement with one another is not to be trifled with either. We should take this seriousness into our interactions with each other. Relationships like this are not some optional appendage on our Christianity. They are at the very core of it, as we have maintained throughout this book.

The Key Word: Spur On

With this seriousness in mind, let us turn our attention to the key word that we are looking at in the passage. In Greek it is *paroxusmos*. In the NIV it is translated "spur on" and in the King James Version, "provoke." Both translations capture the flavor and strength of the Greek word. The Holman CSB waters it down, in our opinion, with "promote" and the New American Standard Bible (NASB), likewise, weakens the idea with "stimulate."

From Baer-Arndt-Gingrich, one of the basic Greek lexicons, we find these meanings:

1) stirring up, provoking—only used here in New Testament
2) irritation, sharp disagreement—only in Acts 15:39
3) attack of a high fever—not in New Testament

Not a lot of information, right? The word is used only two

times in the whole New Testament. Another piece of information: the Greek word is transliterated into English as *paroxysm*, which means according to Webster,

1) a sudden violent outburst
2) a fit of violent action or emotion
3) medically—a severe attack or increase in the violence of a disease

We share this to call attention to the force and intensity of the term. This is not a "nice" word. It is not a calm word. It is an aggressive word. I (Steve) think I can relate a little. As I mentioned in a previous chapter, twenty years ago I suffered through three kidney stones. About a year before the writing of this book, I had a paroxysm—a "severe attack," a "violent outburst" of pain and agony as the kidney stones returned.

The experience motivated both me and the doctor to put me through a series of analysis to determine the cause and figure out what I could do to avoid future adventures with the little rocks. In other words it "spurred me on," it "provoked me," it "stimulated me" to get busy and do something. So are you getting the idea of what the Hebrew writer is telling us to do? This strong language fits totally into the context we talked about earlier. This is an intense word in an intense context.

Two Tempering Ideas

The strength of the concept is tempered by two other ideas in the text. First, we should consider ("notice, contemplate" or—as in the Holman CSB—"be concerned about") how we go about accomplishing the "spurring on." It requires thought. It means we have to contemplate our brother, his needs and his situation, and how to best help him to respond to the Lord. No "cookie-cutter discipleship" here; no "one size fits all" Christianity. We aren't to just blow into someone's life and drop a *paroxysm* on them. We are to give thought, no doubt, prayerful thought to how to best spur them on.

The second tempering idea is the final result expected by our action, which is "love and good works." We have never seen a person inspired to love by screaming or ranting and raving. Unfortunately, we have seen it tried but never seen it work. These verses present the certainty that our words and actions can make a real difference in the outcome of someone's life when guided by consideration.

What Does It Look Like?

Before we get away from this concept, we have to think through some challenging questions: How does this look in real life? How does it play out in our fellowship at church? How do we "spur one another on"? As some of us have learned from Gary Chapman's book *The Five Love Languages,* when it comes to feeling love, we all have different things that communicate love to us.

It is the same way with spurring one another on. What fires me up might be absolutely discouraging to you. So the real test is in the effect produced by our "spurring." The goal, as you remember, is "to promote love and good works." Therefore, we need to figure out ("consider") what works for the people around us, and we need to extend much grace with others who attempt to put this verse into practice in our lives. The very fact that someone cares enough to try to spur me on should in itself do some "spurring."

That said, what are some things we can do or say to spur each other on?

- Pray specifically for another's need, struggle or weakness, and let them know that you are doing so, which also sets you up to ask for an update.
- Share a scripture that you believe will be relevant in their life.
- When someone shares a struggle or burden or sin with you, remember to ask them about it consistently. As we mentioned in chapter 6, the consistent and regular, even daily, connection provides great power to help us grow and overcome.
- Do not be afraid to give someone a bold challenge. After a recent prayer walk with a couple of brothers, I (Tom) told them how inspired I was by their prayers, and I told them I had something very important to say to them. I then took a few minutes to share with them how I believed they needed to aspire to be leaders in God's family and how I wanted to have a part in encouraging that.
- We are not so sure about this for women, but we can well imagine good coming when a brother says to another brother, "Come on, man, we can do so much more to get some guys to come out and hear about Jesus and the kingdom. Let's get off our duffs and bring some people in."
- Just step out and do it. Consider and pray, but do it. If you make a mistake, apologize and learn from it. Let us spur you on!

These ideas, and many, many more that you can supply, are really all about the power of joining together to accomplish God's will and working with each other, instead of struggling to make it on our own. Of course, all of these endeavors to help each other grow will require great wisdom, not to go too far and become offensive and not to hold back and damage others by our negligence.

One more thought before we wrap up this chapter. Not ours—someone else said this, but it rings true:

> It is impossible to stimulate someone else to love and good deeds if we are not around them. We cannot be an encouragement if we live our lives in secret caves, pushing people away from us. People out of touch don't encourage others. Encouragement is a face-to-face thing.[1]

This echoes what the writer of Hebrews said in verse 25.

We have to continue to insist on the corporate nature of NT Christianity. The "it's all about me and my God" idea that is so prevalent in our society is a result of a later aberration of what God intended Christianity to be. He made us to be together, to need each other and to function best when we are working together, "spurring one another on to love and good works."

---

1. Charles R. Swindoll, *Growing Deep in the Christian Life* (Grand Rapids: Zondervan, 1995).

Making It Real

1. Do you see a difference in "spurring" someone on and encouraging them? Explain.
2. What do you think it means when the New Testament uses strong language and words with intense meanings?
3. Let us assume for a minute that you find yourself resenting someone who tries to spur you on because it makes you feel pressured. How would you try to work this out, both with the person and within yourself?
4. In other chapters we have talked about the corollary of some of these NT teachings. The corollary (or companion truth) to the need to spur others on is that we need to be thankful for people who do that in our lives. How do you feel about that?
5. What is some way you can spur someone on this week? Who is the best person for you to focus on?
6. Who can you ask to consistently spur you on?

Reconciling with One Another

The Bible is clear: Jesus came to break down divisions between people. Paul states it clearly in Ephesians 2:14:

> For He is our peace, who made both groups one and tore down the dividing wall of hostility. (HCSB)

The world, on the other hand, specializes in division—whether it is caused by race, money, gender, culture or distance. There is so much to polarize, to divide us, to split us up. And even if we do not succumb to these barriers, then there is lack of time. It seems like we are just too busy to build great, long-lasting friendships; to get close and stay close.

Even in the church there are many barriers to relationships other than the ones already mentioned: past hurts, bitterness, and of course, sin. Whether it is yours, mine or ours, sin divides us, alienates us and builds walls between us.

This is why Jesus is still the only real answer. He broke down the walls that divide and separate us, and he is still in the "breaking down walls" business today:

> [He did this so] that He might reconcile both to God in one body through the cross and put the hostility to death by it. (Ephesians 2:16, HCSB)

The key lesson we have to learn and keep learning about broken or damaged relationships is that reconciliation occurs at the foot of the cross. Like the song says: "Jesus will fix it." This is what he does. He fixes broken relationships. This is his specialty. It does not matter how long the relationship has been broken or how badly it is messed up. He can unite the alienated, rebuild the trust and restore the love. This is what happens at the foot of the cross. A completely holy and righteous God is reunited with his unholy and unrighteous enemy (you and me) through the loving sacrifice of Jesus. See Romans 5:6–11 for a short refresher course on this awesome fact.

Become Friends Again

Another important lesson comes from the very word "reconcile." The basic meaning of the word is "to become friends again." We are not talking about learning to politely tolerate one another, to grudgingly agree to a "ceasefire" in an ongoing battle, or to stiffly interact while bitterness boils beneath the surface. We are talking about the walls coming down in our hearts and minds. The goal Jesus set is to be "one" (John 17:20–21). When we accomplish that goal, we have one of the most powerful testimonies to the validity of our faith.

We also have to remember as we read Ephesians that it was written in the midst of a cultural, racial and ethnic battle that has raged across the centuries. The division between Jew and non-Jew has been so acrimonious that in recent times it spawned not only the Holocaust, where an estimated six million Jews were exterminated, but also the repeated denial by some political figures that the Holocaust ever happened. Reconciliation seems more real when we realize that, in the midst of this race war, a Jew appeared who overcame the division and hate, and molded a unified group of followers by blending Jews and non-Jews into a harmonious whole.

If that kind of hostility could be overcome, anything is possible with God. When Paul prays at the end of Ephesians 3, "Now to him who is able to do immeasurably more than all we ask or imagine, according to his power that is at work within us..." he is most likely, in this context, thinking specifically about God's amazing work of reconciliation.

BIBLICAL PRINCIPLES OF RECONCILIATION

Let us look at some biblical principles that will help us put reconciliation into practice in our lives. You see, although Jesus did the "heavy lifting," so to speak, there still remains much for us to do so that we can meet at the foot of that cross.

1. Realize the urgency and importance of being reconciled.

> "Therefore, if you are offering your gift at the altar and there remember that your brother has something against you, leave your gift there in front of the altar. First go and be reconciled to your brother; then come and offer your gift." (Matthew 5:23–24)

This passage continues to shock us. God would rather we get things patched up with our brother than to come and worship him. This puts getting along with our brothers and sisters in a different light. This is particularly remarkable when you consider all the effort the Jewish worshipper had to make to finally arrive at that altar inside the Court of the Gentiles, inside the Court of the Women and inside the Court of Israel with his approved sacrifice. Have you ever done something like this? Have you called someone on Saturday night to talk so that you can worship God acceptably the next day? This is so urgent, so important that I should not rest until it is taken care of. Do you need to stop reading this chapter right now and go work out a conflict?

2. Accept the obligation and possibility of reconciliation.

The encouraging part of the Matthew 5:23–24 text is realizing that God expects us to do it and then to pick back up where we left off. Jesus does not contemplate years of counseling or much prayer and fasting. He just says go "be reconciled." We overcomplicate things. Go. Apologize. Forgive. Then get back to worship, maybe this time together.

3. Know that we cannot always have our way.

> As a prisoner for the Lord, then, I urge you to live a life worthy of the calling you have received. Be completely humble and gentle; be patient, bearing with one another in love. (Ephesians 4:1–2)

> Bear with each other and forgive whatever grievances you may have against one another. Forgive as the Lord forgave you. (Colossians 3:13)

These passages bring in what I (Steve) like to call the "putting up with" factor. In the kingdom of God none of us is the king, and we are all very different. We have different socioeconomic backgrounds; we come from different races; we have different education levels, even different cultures. I love the diversity, but it does make it challenging to understand each other and accept one another. My coauthor, Tom, calls it the "hanging in there" factor. Whatever we may call it, reconciliation does not mean that everybody will agree with me or that what we call "church" should be characterized by uniformity. The power of the gospel is best seen in diversity working together in harmony.

4. Make every effort to work things out.

> Make every effort to keep the unity of the Spirit through the bond of peace. (Ephesians 4:3)

"Well, I tried to talk to so and so, but it didn't work." Try again. And again. And again. Pray. Get help. Try again. Make every effort. Do everything within your power.

5. Forgive.

> Bear with each other and forgive whatever grievances you may have against one another. Forgive as the Lord forgave you. (Colossians 3:13)

I (Steve) have been married almost thirty-three years to my lovely wife, Diane. We started off as best friends and have tried to maintain that friendship through all the ups and downs of life. I do not recall where we first learned the importance of taking time to end some little bit of conflict by saying "I'm sorry" and "I forgive you." We insisted our kids learn to say it. We shared it with all the couples we counseled. There is power in verbalizing it. Those few words can be amazingly hard to utter. And having to do so often prolonged some discussions until we were ready to ask for and extend forgiveness.

6. Pray.

> But I tell you, love your enemies and pray for those who persecute you. (Matthew 5:44)

If Jesus instructs us to pray for our enemies, which totally goes against our human nature, how much more should we be praying for our brothers and sisters, especially when we are not getting along? Pray for them, for their hearts, and pray for you and your heart.

EXAMPLES OF CONFLICTS IN THE BIBLE

Paul and Barnabas

> After some time had passed, Paul said to Barnabas, "Let's go back and visit the brothers in every town where we have preached the message of the Lord, and see how they're doing." Barnabas wanted to take along John Mark. But Paul did not think it appropriate to take along this man who had deserted them in Pamphylia and had not gone on with them to the work. There was such a sharp disagreement that they parted company, and Barnabas took Mark with him and sailed off to Cyprus. Then Paul chose Silas and departed, after being commended to the grace of the Lord by the brothers. He traveled through Syria and Cilicia, strengthening the churches. (Acts 15:36–40, HCSB)

We somewhat reluctantly include this passage because it has often been used and abused, meaning that it deserves a more detailed treatment than we have time for. These verses have even been used to justify dividing the body of Christ.

So first of all, let us try to just stick to the facts. Fact #1: Paul and Barnabas had a sharp disagreement about a ministry decision (not a biblical or doctrinal dispute). Fact #2: Both continued to work for God. Fact #3: Both returned to the mission but in different directions with different partners. Fact #4: Paul was commended by the brothers. We have to be careful how we argue from silence here. Just because the writer does not mention that Barnabas was also commended, does not prove that Paul was right and Barnabas was wrong. Fact #5: There was no bitterness or lasting disruption of fellowship. (See Colossians 4:10 and 2 Timothy 4:11.)

So what lessons can we learn from this story that will help us deal with damaged relationships?

- Christians can have sharp disagreements and remain Christ-like in their conduct and maintain their relationships.
- Time can change things—such as Paul's thinking about John Mark. Because of John Mark's past actions, Paul had not trusted him, but later he recognized his usefulness to him in the ministry. (Again see Colossians 4:10 and 2 Timothy 4:11.) Who grew? Was it John Mark who matured or was it Paul? The Bible does not say.
- This passage does not excuse destroying relationships, harboring ill will or justifying division.

Euodia and Syntyche

> I urge Euodia and I urge Syntyche to agree in the Lord. Yes, I also ask you, true partner, to help these women who have contended for the gospel at my side, along with Clement and the rest of my coworkers whose names are in the book of life. (Philippians 4:2–3, HCSB)

We can learn some basic lessons from this little tidbit that Paul saw fit to include in a letter to his friends in the church in Philippi. First, conflict happens. It is a normal part of any healthy relationship. Both of us have had to learn this in our marriages. Conflict is a normal part of growing closer. In itself it is not bad. Its ultimate effect depends on our response to it. Remember "iron sharpens iron" (Proverbs 27:17). Second, the goal is to agree. Third, we may need help from a third party. This may be the most important lesson of all. If we are not getting along, then get help!

David and Saul

The story found in 1 Samuel 24:8–22 of the troubled and turbulent relationship between the insanely jealous King Saul and David, the one God designated to replace him, teaches us a valuable lesson about relationships. There is only so much one person can do because, as the saying goes, "It takes two to tango." David's conduct with Saul was above reproach. He did everything he could to work out his relationship with Saul. And in the end he remarkably avoided anger or bitterness toward someone who rejected him to the point of continually trying to kill him. (Remember David's response to Saul's death in 2 Samuel 1.)

Paul puts it this way in Romans 12:18: "If it is possible, as far as it depends on you, live at peace with everyone." He indicates that there is much we can do, but that having peace in any given relationship requires both parties to desire it. Obviously there is no excuse in this passage for not doing everything we can, nor is it an open door to a bitterness that will eat us alive. It puts forth the truth that if one of us changes, the relationship changes. Paul reminds us that there are things that do depend on us, things that we have control over, that we can do something about. Then it becomes up to the other person to respond in kind.

SOME THINGS DEPEND UPON US

1. We can always have a gracious attitude.

> Some, to be sure, preach Christ out of envy and strife, but others out of good will. These do so out of love, knowing that I am appointed for the defense of the gospel; the others proclaim Christ out of rivalry, not sincerely, seeking to cause [me] trouble in my imprisonment. What does it matter? Just that in every way, whether out of false motives or

true, Christ is proclaimed. And in this I rejoice. Yes, and I will rejoice because I know this will lead to my deliverance through your prayers and help from the Spirit of Jesus Christ. (Philippians 1:15–19, HCSB)

Paul's spirit here is incredible, is it not? Even though his so-called brothers are preaching the gospel motivated by a desire to stir up more trouble for him, Paul chooses to focus on the result—Christ is being proclaimed—and not on the wrong motivation that prompts it.

2. We can always be humble.

Do nothing out of rivalry or conceit, but in humility consider others as more important than yourselves. Everyone should look out not [only] for his own interests, but also for the interests of others. (Philippians 2:3–4, HCSB)

I, therefore, the prisoner in the Lord, urge you to walk worthy of the calling you have received, with all humility and gentleness, with patience, accepting one another in love. (Ephesians 4:1–2, HCSB)

3. We can always be positive.

Do everything without grumbling and arguing, so that you may be blameless and pure, children of God who are faultless in a crooked and perverted generation, among whom you shine like stars in the world. (Philippians 2:14–15, HCSB)

4. We can always listen.

My dearly loved brothers, understand this: everyone must

be quick to hear, slow to speak, and slow to anger, for man's anger does not accomplish God's righteousness. (James 1:19–20, HCSB)

5. We can always control our anger.

For man's anger does not bring about the righteous life that God desires. (James 1:20)

Conclusion

I (Tom) want to share a memory. I knew a couple thirty-five years ago who had been married more than fifty years at that time. One day I said, "Jake, tell me, when you and Aileen have a conflict, how do you work it through?" He did not hesitate a moment before saying, "Why we never have a conflict."

Now, you can think what you want about his reply, but I share it here to say that his response is not true of most relationships that I know of that have to endure the test of time. We can learn to reduce conflicts, but we know of no way for us to eliminate conflicts.

However, conflicts can become opportunities to grow spiritually as well as occasions to deepen relationships. Both happen when we handle conflicts God's way. The advice from James (here quoted from The Message Bible) can hardly be improved upon:

> Do you want to be counted wise, to build a reputation for wisdom? Here's what you do: Live well, live wisely, live humbly. It's the way you live, not the way you talk, that counts. Mean-spirited ambition isn't wisdom. Boasting that you are wise isn't wisdom. Twisting the truth to make your-

selves sound wise isn't wisdom. It's the furthest thing from wisdom—it's animal cunning, devilish conniving. Whenever you're trying to look better than others or get the better of others, things fall apart and everyone ends up at the others' throats.

Real wisdom, God's wisdom, begins with a holy life and is characterized by getting along with others. It is gentle and reasonable, overflowing with mercy and blessings, not hot one day and cold the next, not two-faced. You can develop a healthy, robust community that lives right with God and enjoy its results only if you do the hard work of getting along with each other, treating each other with dignity and honor. (James 3:14–18, The Message)

Making It Real

1. Do you have broken relationships in the church? In your family? In your part of the world?
2. What are your feelings about seeking reconciliation?
3. Look at the items under "Some Things Depend upon Us" and evaluate how you are doing in each of these areas.

12

Forgiving One Another

The New Testament paints a picture of God's plan for those who live under a new covenant. On the canvas we see disciples of Jesus fully engaged in relationships with each other, committed to unity, following the example of their leader in laying down their lives for each other. Their goal in every relationship is to be completely humble and open to others' input. Their thinking is much more focused on "what can we do for one another" than on "what is the best for me." Now that they have been born again, they love one another deeply from the heart.

But as we noted in chapter 7, Scripture is realistic. Look at four rather diverse passages that all recognize the reality that even the most serious followers will sin against each other.

SINNING AGAINST EACH OTHER

Matthew 18:32–33

> "Then the master called the servant in. 'You wicked servant," he said, 'I canceled all that debt of yours because you begged me to. Shouldn't you have had mercy on your fellow servant just as I had on you?' In anger his master turned him over to the jailers to be tortured, until he should pay back all he owed.

> "This is how my heavenly Father will treat each of you unless you forgive your brother from your heart."

Ephesians 4:32–5:2

> Be kind and compassionate to one another, forgiving each other, just as in Christ God forgave you. Be imitators of God, therefore, as dearly loved children and live a life of love, just as Christ loved us and gave himself up for us as a fragrant offering and sacrifice to God.

Colossians 3:13

> Bear with each other and forgive whatever grievances you may have against one another. Forgive as the Lord forgave you.

1 Peter 4:8

> Above all, love each other deeply, because love covers over a multitude of sins.

In spite of our commitment and determination to be faithful to each other, we will still sin. And so the Scriptures spell out how we are to handle those situations when the beautiful picture is blemished or shattered. Husbands and wives, family members and members of the body of Christ will all sin.

Whenever it occurs, sin hurts, sin damages, and sin separates. So how do we handle it? In the end, after all is said and done, we must forgive one another. Let us examine six matters related to forgiveness.

ABOUT FORGIVENESS

1. Forgiveness often is not easy.

For the most part, sin that is against us or the body of Christ causes pain. That rude insult pierces us. That unfaithfulness causes anger and sadness. Deception and dishonesty just hurt. Pain makes an impression and creates a lasting memory. It is hard to let go of. The more deliberate the sin seems to be or the more we have invested in the relationship, the greater the pain it usually causes. The greater the pain, the harder it is to forgive.

2. Forgiveness may be hardest to give in the church.

Here we have much higher expectations of each other, and so we ask, "How could my brother/sister do that and hurt us that much?" When we are involved more deeply in the body, we often have more opportunities to see each other's flaws and experience our "dark sides." We expect certain things from friends and family in the world, but when we see sin in our brothers and sisters in Christ, there seems to be a much greater temptation to bitterness.

3. Satan's top-ranked scheme may be to lead us not to forgive.

Most of us know that the Scripture teaches that Satan has schemes. We sometimes talk about how he designs them just for us in a most unique way. But have you ever noticed the context of the passage that talks about Satan's schemes?

> The reason I wrote you was to see if you would stand the test and be obedient in everything. If you forgive anyone, I also forgive him. And what I have forgiven—if there was anything to forgive—I have forgiven in the sight of Christ for your sake, in order that Satan might not outwit us. For we are not unaware of his schemes. (2 Corinthians 2:9–11)

Satan surely has other schemes, but if he can keep us from forgiving each other, it will not matter how much time and energy we have poured into building our relationships. If he can get us to forget the cross and what saves us and to apply a different standard or model to our brothers and sisters, he can celebrate his victory. Sin can blemish the body of Christ. But given what has been done for us, there is no uglier blemish than the one caused by the lack of forgiveness. That would seem to be the import of Jesus' parable in Matthew 18, quoted in part above.

We are the ten-million-dollar debtor who made a servant's wage of seventeen cents a day and had no hope of paying off the debt. We would just have needed 186,000 years under the best and unrealistic conditions! "Give me just a little more time" indeed! You can see where Jesus goes with this. When the forgiven man himself will not forgive, it is appalling. Such a sin is not just a violation of God's will; it undermines the very core of the gospel and the heart of the kingdom. (This parable was, after all, about the kingdom.)

When we have an attitude that says, "I am just not ready to forgive him yet," we must ask ourselves, "What is it going to take?" Do we not stand amazed at how much God has not only forgiven us, but what a place of honor he has given us at his table? When we find ourselves saying, "I'm just not sure I am ready to forgive yet," the next words out of our mouths should be, "God be merciful to me a sinner" or "Lord Jesus, have mercy on me."

For those who have been massively forgiven to miserly ration out forgiveness on their emotional timetable is shocking and disturbing. Yes, it may take us some time to get our emotions fully engaged in forgiveness, but there should be no doubt that we know this is where we must go and will go.

The church is not a place where we will not sin against each other and will not need to forgive one another. The church is a place where forgiveness must be demonstrated and evident for all to see. Knowing this, Satan will work in whatever devious ways he can to encourage us to hold to bitterness or anger.

James 3:14 says, "But if you harbor bitter envy and selfish ambition in your hearts, do not boast about it or deny the truth." To harbor a ship for the winter meant to leave it there for a long period. If we harbor bitterness, we are holding on to it instead of cutting the moorings and letting it go.

4. Forgiveness is the ultimate 'one another' trump card.

Brothers and sisters may make various mistakes and foolishly commit many sins. The cards they play against God, the body and against us may grow to be quite a stack, but love, which always forgives, can trump all of them and cover a multitude of sins (1 Peter 4:8). In appendix 2 we have material discussing what the church must do when there is ongoing sin that is not repented of. But a person's failure to be embraced by the body must always come because of their lack of repentance, never because of our lack of love and forgiveness.

5. Forgiveness must come from a grateful heart.

Forgiveness must be much more than a duty or obedience to a command. When this is all it is, it has the potential of being offered in a condescending manner with a self-righteous spirit or without a full embrace of the one being forgiven.

When we are the one being asked to forgive, there is a tendency to see ourselves in a one-up position and the other person in one-down position. If we see it that way, we can sinfully relish our position and want the other person to squirm a bit as they wait for our decision. If forgiveness comes from anything else other than the gratitude in our own hearts for our forgiveness, we lack purity of heart. Paul gives us the right motive for forgiveness:

> Get rid of all bitterness, rage and anger, brawling and slander, along with every form of malice. Be kind and compassionate to one another, forgiving each other, just as in Christ God forgave you. (Ephesians 4:31–32)

We are to forgive just as the servant in Jesus' parable was to forgive, because of how grateful we are for the multitude of sins for which God has forgiven us.

6. We must help one another forgive.

It is not unusual to find a brother or sister struggling with forgiveness. They feel hurt and disappointed. They are tempted to say, "I would not have done that." They may be right, and the wrong done to them may be ugly. But they stand in the place of the Pharisee who prayed about himself. Bitterness develops in them, and they may want the other person to have more pain. Every conversation may reveal a resentful and bitter heart. But think about the principles we have already studied.

We are to teach and admonish one another. If we overtake someone in a sin, we are to restore them gently and then help them carry that burden out of their life. We are to spur one another on to love and good deeds.

When a person is not forgiving, they grow bitter—a sin, ironically, that may eclipse the sin they will not forgive in another. If ever anyone needs our help, it is someone who is not forgiving. If we stand by and let them hold on to their bitterness or their grudge, it is like standing by while someone points a loaded gun at their head. And God forbid that we would do anything to justify the person (e.g., "You have every right to feel the way you do") and offer support to their bitterness. No, we must heed the words found in Hebrews 12:

> Make every effort to live in peace with all men and to be holy; without holiness no one will see the Lord. See to it that no one misses the grace of God and that no bitter root grows up to cause trouble and defile many. (Hebrews 12:14–15)

We must take our friend by the hand, literally or figuratively, and walk them gently to the foot of the cross where we can together meditate and pray. There is no sin we cannot forgive wholeheartedly and generously when we see clearly how he who knew no sin, became sin, so that in him we might become the righteousness of God. It may take a while to help our friend get there. Pain and anger are not resolved in a moment, but let us never doubt where we must end up.

If forgiveness cannot be found in the church of Jesus Christ, where can it be found? Those of us who stand at the foot of the cross and the towering mountains of grace, must bear witness to the gospel by the way we forgive one another.

Making It Real

1. Why should forgiveness be one of the most fundamental aspects in our relationships with one another?

2. Why is forgiveness often such a real struggle for us?

3. Where are you most struggling with forgiveness right now and why?

4. What biblical truth do you need to most embrace to move forward and forgive?

5. What is something you have learned that has helped you forgive?

13

'One Another' in Groups

On the night this was written I (Tom) was on one of my writing retreats that I have gone on for almost every book I have written. I can get so much more done when I have just one focus for about forty-eight hours without any distractions. While I was writing, a small group was meeting in my home. I seldom miss our meetings and thank God for the way I see the types of relationships we are writing about coming alive in that group. Steve could say the same thing about his group, which he *was* able to be part of on this same night.

We have given particular emphasis in this book to the Greek word *allelon*—one another. While some of the things we have examined are better practiced one-on-one, "one another" does not just mean one-on-one. We do not function in relationships one-on-one only, but often in small groups.

The small group was the center of Jesus' ministry. Think about how much time he spent with just the twelve. The small group will always be crucial in our life together in Christ and will be where body life is most personally experienced. Any church that does not have some kind of small group arrangement should work to change that as soon as possible. That being true, it seems good to look at biblical principles for group dynamics. Before you continue, we would suggest that you read the following texts, all from Paul's writings.

- Romans 12:5-13
- 1 Corinthians 12:21-26
- Ephesians 4:1-13
- 1 Thessalonians 5:10-28
- Colossians 4:2-6

Groups can be chaotic or harmonious, boring or exciting, healthy or dysfunctional, productive or wasteful. Though hours of research have been spent in the corporate and academic world searching for the ways to make groups function most effectively, one will not find principles anywhere that so consistently produce healthy groups like those you just read about in these passages. Groups of disciples are not always healthy, but it is never because Scripture does not provide the needed guidance.

SEVEN PRINCIPLES

We will focus here on seven principles derived from these texts that will cause a great dynamic in your group when you practice them and call others to practice them. If you are a group leader, your first task is to model these principles yourself and then to help your group understand them. If you are a group member, you need to understand that your commitment to these will make a difference in the spiritual health of the group.

1. Focus on 'belonging' and being 'devoted' (Romans 12:5, 10).

In this group you all belong to one another. You are "members one of another" some translations say. This is a group of disciples of Jesus, not the garden club. This is the family of God, not the Rotary Club. This is an outcropping of the kingdom of God, not just people you go to a meeting with. These are those with whom you have been united with Christ. This is your spiritual family—right now at this point in your life, your most immediate spiritual family. Consider all that belonging means to you, and from that sense of belonging, be devoted to the group. Do not just expect the leader to do that.

Be a giver, not just a taker. Consider the needs. In every group there is always a need for great listeners. We do not mean here people who are just quiet. We mean active listeners who ask questions and draw people out. A book was written years ago titled *The Awesome Power of the Listening Ear*.[1] We do tap into a needed relational power when we listen with our heads and our hearts. Part of being a giver means to give your ears to others. How would your friends rate you as a listener? Do you want to make changes?

Take responsibility for how you affect the group. Do your part to make the group warm, loving, supportive, open, zealous, prayerful. Pray that God will use you—yes, you—to inspire the group for his sake.

If you find your focus drifting to "I'm not getting much out of this group," check your heart and your actions. Are you showing up, mooching and feeling entitled, or are you belonging, devoted and giving?

2. Appreciate, affirm and encourage the different gifts (Romans 12:5–8, 1 Corinthians 12).

Be sure that you first open your eyes and see the diversity in your group. You can see this even if your group is made up of seven black men named Johnson. We are all so distinctive. God made us and then gave us spiritual gifts so that we are all unique. Be a person who appreciates this and looks for ways to encourage others as they use their gifts.

In the church where we two authors are members, we did a sermon series on the theme of "Enjoying." On one Sunday, we

---

1. John W. Drakeford, *The Awesome Power of the Listening Ear* (Nashville: Word Books, 1987).

emphasized the fact that God has given us our brothers and sisters for our enjoyment. Yes, there will be challenges, but do not miss the opportunity to enjoy your group, the diversity in it and the special things that each person can bring to it.

When addressing the diversity in the body, Scripture goes out of the way to emphasize the "weaker parts." We should do the same thing. Be sure to give special focus to those who may feel marginalized by illness or some form of disability. Be alert for anyone who feels they do not have much to give or wonder what their place is and help them see that by the power of God they have much to give. Giving special honor to the weak is the way of Jesus and the kingdom of God.

3. Look for the Spirit's work in all things (1 Thess. 5:16-19).

The Spirit is always at work (John 5:17, Romans 8:28). Be watchful and alert. Do not put out his fire through your faithlessness or negativity. Be expectant, eager to see what he is going to do next in your group.

Let us give an example. Suppose you have what seems to be the perfect small group—a picture of diversity and harmony. But then one couple has to move to another city and soon another couple or single person comes in to your group, also the result of a move. Suddenly, the group seems thrown off. It just doesn't have the same good feel it once had. You can whine, "I liked our group the way it was" (and that will surely encourage everyone!), or you can ask, "What is the Spirit doing? What is he wanting to teach us, and especially me?"

Whatever happens, it is an opportunity for the Spirit to work. Learn to focus not on the problem, but on the opportunity presented and on the Spirit, who never finds a situation in which he cannot work.

Guard against the natural tendency to look at your group through unspiritual eyes, only seeing the ordinariness of the people and their blemishes and weaknesses. Remember Paul's words:

> But God chose the foolish things of the world to shame the wise; God chose the weak things of the world to shame the strong. He chose the lowly things of this world and the despised things—and the things that are not—to nullify the things that are, so that no one may boast before him. (1 Corinthians 1:27–29)

What Paul describes could only be accomplished by the work of the Spirit. Be fascinated with how the Spirit will take your "lowly" group and use it to shame Satan's strong and mighty legions.

Also guard against looking at your group with unspiritual eyes and seeking to only spend time with those you naturally "click" with. God wants to teach us through people who are different from us. And he wants us to learn to love each other.

4. Support leadership (1 Thessalonians 5:12–13).

No group can function very long or with effectiveness without leadership, and God has ordained that there be leaders in his church. Leaders must always be discussed when we talk about group dynamics. Not all leadership is handled in a godly way, but the concept of leadership is godly.

In this passage in 1 Thessalonians Paul speaks of showing respect to those who are "over you in the Lord." He goes further saying, "Hold them in the highest regard in love because of their work." This is a clear call to support leadership. Paul does not say if he is referring to a particular role of leadership, such as the elders, but shouldn't everyone who leads, organizes, prepares and cares be shown the highest regard because of their work? One way to guarantee a dysfunctional group is to have group members who feel free to withhold their support from the leader. This sends vibes through the whole group and will usually influence others. It lays the groundwork for divisiveness.

Most leaders do what Paul says in 1 Thessalonians 5: they work hard among us. Leaders are just people. If you are not currently a leader, you may have been one, or you may someday be one. Leaders are just like everyone else—they need encouragement. Leadership can often feel like a pretty thankless job. One of the most helpful things you can do for your group is to ask your leader if he/she feels your support and encouragement and to ask how you can more fully show it.

This does not mean you have to agree with everything a leader does and does not mean you just stuff any feelings and thoughts you have. On the contrary, the only healthy dynamic occurs when we talk things out with a leader and work through differences we may have. If you ever need to bring a third party in for this kind of time, do not hesitate to do it, which leads to our next principle. But do not forget God's plan: support leadership unless doing so causes you to compromise convictions, and even then you can maintain a submissive and respectful spirit.

5. Work out differences; maintain unity (Ephesians 4:1-7, 15).

Do you remember those seven black guys all named Johnson? Just as they will all be unique, they will also not think exactly alike even as they follow the same Jesus and read the same Bible. Mix in some women and some Anglos and some Latinos and some Asians, and you have even more different perspectives, opinions and conclusions. Every group—no matter how homogeneous or how diverse—will have to deal with differences. This is why chapter 11 in this book deals with reconciling with each other.

Do not be surprised when there are differences. Peter and Paul had them. Even the affable and encouraging Barnabas had them with Paul. See differences as an opportunity—an opportunity for the Spirit to work, an opportunity for iron to sharpen iron, and especially an opportunity for us to go to the cross and practice humility. But whatever happens, have Jesus' passion for unity.

6. Be sensitive to outsiders; seek to bring them 'in' (Col. 4:2-6).

For Christians, the discussion of group dynamics must include reference to outsiders. In many situations we are seeking to have them come into our midst, where we hope they see relationships that proclaim that the kingdom of God is among us.

"Be wise in the way you act toward outsiders," writes Paul. "Make the most of every opportunity." When outsiders are among us, the dynamic of the group needs to change. We do not mean we need to put on a front. We do not mean that we need to stop being transparent. What we mean is that we need to avoid behavior and "in house" lingo that would make the outsider really feel like an outsider. Something that is just fine to say when only the group members are present may leave our visiting friend feeling like he does not know the "secret handshake," so he may not want to come back.

Talk this over in your group. Discuss the most genuine and sensitive way to interact when non-Christians or even Christians not from your fellowship are among you.

7. Stay at the foot of the cross.

When you think about it, you may want to move this to the top of the list, or you may want to make it the first thing you think about and the point you end with. What makes a Christian group different from any other is the cross, and when you take the cross out of a Christian group, it begins to look like all the other groups in the world (just look at the church in Corinth). Whenever a group is not functioning as it should, or being inspiring and encouraging as it should, the first question we should ask is, "Where is this group in regard to the cross?" Are we living the baptized life? Are we dying and rising with Jesus? Where has "self" slipped in? More personally we should ask ourselves, in relationship to this group, "Where am I in regard to the cross?"

Each small group of Jesus' disciples can be a microcosm of the kingdom of God. Each group can be the scene of the Spirit's work. Let us be thankful for those fellow pilgrims God gives us to travel with, and let us have the attitudes needed to live for God and one another.

Making It Real

1. If you were on trial for being devoted to your small group, what evidence would be presented to convict you?
2. Write out the different gifts and strengths found in your group. Is there a "weaker" person who needs special encouragement?
3. What is happening now in your group that could very well be an opportunity for the Spirit to work (maybe in a surprising way)?
4. Ask the leader of your group if he or she feels your support and encouragement. Pray the Spirit will work in this conversation.
5. Is there any issue that you need to resolve with anyone in the group?
6. Ask others how they feel about your interaction in the group.
7. Do you need to talk with anyone in your group about being appropriate and wise with outsiders?
8. How does everything in this chapter and in this book converge at the cross? Where are you in relation to the cross?

The Logical Conclusion: Let Us Begin

By now we would hope that you are thoroughly convinced that building close relationships, experiencing *koinonia,* and being united with disciples in ways that encourage our transformation is what kingdom living is all about.

We would hope you could never be satisfied just attending church or hopping around from one congregation to another to meet your own needs. We would hope you are determined to live the baptized life among a people you can know and who will know you—showing the world what disciples and the kingdom of God are all about. That, we hope, will be the logical conclusion of this study for you.

A Practical Conclusion

But here is the truth: none of this will mean much if we are not able to move from a logical conclusion to a practical conclusion. To say it another way, we may figure out well enough how to talk the talk, but it means nothing at all unless we walk the talk. A great theology of relationships is a good start, even a crucial one, but the word must become flesh. And so the real logical conclusion is that there must be a practical, real life application of these great principles and directives from God.

The good news is that none of us has to wait for some church program to be launched to either get started or go deeper in our relationships. Today you can pray about something you have studied here and then make a phone call, send an e-mail, drive over to someone's house or pull aside with someone at a church meeting and strike the match that lights the fire that will become what D. Elton Trueblood once called "the incendiary fellowship." He was talking about the fellowship where the Spirit's fire is not being put out and where the gifts of God are being fanned into flame through relationships.

All of us can start right where we are. All of us have a match in our hands. The words from John F. Kennedy's inaugural address come to mind:

> All this will not be finished in the first one hundred days.
>
> Nor will it be finished in the first one thousand days; nor in the life of this Administration; nor even perhaps in our lifetime on this planet. But let us begin.

Where to Begin?

But where exactly should we begin? The answer will depend on where we have been. Some of us have been seeking these kinds of relationships for many years. That, however, does not guarantee that we have them now or that we have them like we did fifteen years ago. Changes, circumstances and conditions all take their toll on us. We drift. We tire. We sin. Entropy does not just apply to science. A marriage, a friendship and a church's fellowship can all begin to move away from something healthy to something not as healthy. It is a natural tendency.

If this has happened to us, we can celebrate again that the Bible contains this great life-saving word called "repentance." Our love and zeal can be rekindled. We can do the things we did before (Revelation 2:5). And so if this is where you have been, start by remembering those things that led to deep relationships, and do them again. Set up those regular meetings, let someone really help you know and guard your heart, initiate those prayer times, let confession be part of your walk, show up at unexpected times just to encourage, get another person and go out and be bold about your faith, and do those things that create special memories. You can think of more, but whatever you do, just make sure you do not let comfort control you; let Christ control you. Let us begin.

If your relationships seem to reflect many things we have talked about in this book, praise God for his grace that has brought you this far. But do not get complacent. Face the sobering fact that as good as it may seem to be for you, you have only just begun. Our model is the relationship that the Father, Son and Spirit have. How do you describe that? We have further to go. "Miles to go before we sleep." Pray that you will go further. Then realize that going further will almost certainly mean some suffering.

Sometimes we hear, "Be careful what you pray for." It is probably better to say, "Be ready to embrace what you pray for, knowing it will test you and make you better, your relationships better and other people better." Look to Jesus; ask for his mercy. But let us begin.

If you are a new Christian, maybe with your hair still a bit wet from the water of baptism, this is such a new world for you. Hopefully you have seen in the lives of the friends who helped you get to Christ much of what we have talked about. Where do you begin? With a spirit that we actually need to keep our whole lives—the spirit of a grateful, humble learner. Study carefully the passages your mentor(s) give you. But just as importantly, watch their lives. Imitate their faith and their sacrifice. Look at the commitment they have to you, and start looking for ways to make that kind of commitment to another person. Launch out. Do not fear making mistakes. Make some. Just learn from them. Do not underestimate the effect the youngest Christians can have on the fellowship. You have some special matches to start some fires.

Wherever we are, let us begin.

If This Is a New Teaching

But let us speak to one more group. Some of you reading this have been worshipping Jesus and wanting to follow him for a long time, but what you have read here is something you have seldom heard taught, and except for a few of the commands or principles, you have not seen them practiced.

People in your congregation may belong to the church more like they belong to the PTA. Most of them do not know much about each other's lives. Thankfully, they help bear financial burdens and visit the sick, but knowing each other's sins and bearing those to a point of victory is a foreign idea. Having someone in your life who knows your heart and helps you not let it be hardened by sin's deceitfulness may be unheard of in your church culture. If you were to try to be that kind of help to someone else, you have no idea how it would be taken.

So what do you do? Where do you begin? We will not try to give any simplistic or glib answer to this question. There will be many factors to consider. But wherever we are, there is always a right and spiritual way to think, and, thus, a right place to begin. We can only offer some guidance to help you.

As you have seen in this book, our relationship with other disciples is a first-rate, center-of-the-target teaching. If we are going to be Christians, we can no more ignore this than we can ignore our own relationship with God. If we do not want this (and want it all), then we do not really want God's plan. We want something else entirely. As hard as it may be to hear, we want a form of religion that reassures us but fits with our comfort level and our desire.

In our experience—which comes from about seventy-five collective years of church ministry, including our counseling, conversations, reading and observations—we are led to say that the message we have taught here as a major NT emphasis is given marginal attention in most churches, and something far less than central focus in most of the remaining ones. Churches may have dozens of programs and a high level of activity, but so often we have observed that an active member can have things going on in his or her life that desperately need attention. However, nobody knows, or if people do know, they do not apply the biblical principles that would motivate them to get involved. In many cases the person who desperately needs a biblical relationship where "iron sharpens iron" and where one bears the burdens of another is the lead minister or pastor, or some other key leader. And so we read of high-profile leaders who fall from grace. How many more silent sufferers do we never hear about?

If we have described you or the church you attend, please understand us. We do not write to condemn you. We write because we want you to find what Jesus really has in store for you. You may find great comfort and help in your faith right now, but please be open to what God has planned, even if it has not been a part of your church tradition or church culture. If this does describe you, you have the toughest challenge. If these truths become your convictions, you will be swimming against the tide. But take heart—this is when God does his greatest works.

So where do you begin? In prayer at the foot of the cross, saying, "Father, not my will but yours be done." In prayer, asking for courage to just take the next step. In prayer, seeking the best person for you to talk with. In prayer, saying, "Father, help me never quit searching until I find the kind of deep involvement with other Christians that you want me to have." We could say more, but let us all begin regardless of where we are.

What Should a Church Do?

We can all begin. We can all start a fire. With all this being true and exciting, we do feel we need to address something else. While we can all individually make a difference wherever we are, God has planned for Christians to function in groups, in churches (communities of Jesus). It is his plan for those churches to corporately represent who he is. When you spend a little time with a congregation, you get a feel. There is an atmosphere. There is a church culture. There are certain things that are emphasized. There are certain things people are comfortable with and certain other things they are uncomfortable with.

That being true, there is no doubt that the posture of the church and the culture of the church will either encourage or discourage biblical relationships. So while individuals are responsible for being righteous in relationships, decisions by church leaders who set the tone and direction for the church will either encourage or discourage a flourishing of biblical relationships and the practice of the "one another" concepts.

Here is the challenge faced by a number of church leaders that we know. They agree wholeheartedly with what we have presented here. They would fully endorse this statement: "Every disciple of Jesus is to live a 'one-another' life, connected to other Christians and involved with them in ways that are transforming."

They want to move this to the center of the church's life. But how do they best do it? We see several options. To make this a little more interesting and easy to understand, we will use a narrative approach, describing three fictional churches. In listening to our telling of the story you will detect a bit of a bias.

In our scenario the leaders of all three churches examined the Scriptures and determined that the best way to fulfill God's plan for relationships was for every Christian to be a part of a small group. Beyond that they came to some different conclusions.

THREE FICTIONAL EXAMPLES

The Sierra Vista Church

At Sierra Vista the leaders were convinced that they needed a definite plan in place to accomplish something Scripture so highly values. Elder Armando Garza put it this way:

> "The church for a long time has recognized the responsibility we have for educating our people in the Bible, and so we organize and offer classes and ask some people to teach. We ask the whole church to support the program. There are other ways it could be done, but we ask everyone to get behind the plan we all agreed on.
>
> "In the same way we have a responsibility to nurture relationships. Those 'see to it' passages in Hebrews get my attention. And so again, we need to come up with a plan and ask the people to support it. We can't afford to leave this to chance. If we do, it just won't happen."

When the leaders of this church examined all the related scriptures, they saw that some of the things to be done could much better be accomplished when you have a consistent relationship with at least one other person that causes both people to know each other well. They were thinking especially about these ideas: (a) speak the truth in love, (b) bear one another's burden [of sin], (c) teach and admonish one another, (d) confess your sins to one another, and even (e) encourage one another daily so you will not be hardened by sin's deceitfulness. Knowing how important it would be for the relationships to reach these levels, they decided to organize a "one another disciples" plan in which they assigned people to be partners with one another for at least a year. With a congregation of 550 it took the elders, evangelists and women's leaders many hours (and phone calls) to think through what was best. There were so many issues to consider. The process was a bit exhausting.

It was finally finished. From the evangelist and elders down to the newest Christian in the teen ministry, they had every name on a schematic. There was a night of teaching on the subject for the whole church. They then presented the detailed plan to the small group leaders who then talked with the people in their small groups. Knowing there was some hurt from abuses in "discipling partner relationships" in the past, Armando encouraged people to emphasize the "one another" nature of these relationships and not see this as anyone having authority over anyone else.

The Saratoga Church

Though they shared many of the same convictions of the Sierra Vista Church, the leaders here did not feel it best to designate who a person should be partnered with. They knew that a more volunteer approach would likely mean that some people would fall through the cracks, but they felt it was enough exercise of their leadership to say to the church, "We are convinced it is best for every one of us to have someone we can meet with regularly and communicate with often as we practice this call to be with one another."

To discuss and do more teaching, the church held a special meeting. "We want to ask all of you in your small groups to talk this over," said evangelist Donte Brown, "and work out a plan to partner with someone for the next year in order to live out God's call for us to be involved with one another. We realize that there will be many other people you will also be involved with, and thank God for that. But we believe each of us will be blessed by having one person we are clearly partnered with. We do ask that you let your small group leader know who you are connected with, so that the leaders of the church might make sure no one is left out. We are always open to better ways of doing things, but we would ask you to be fully supportive of these efforts."

The Northport Church

The leaders of this church were just as convinced of the relationship principles as their sister congregations. All of them, and especially the evangelist, Wayne Johnson, were committed to keeping these themes before the congregation. It was also agreed that small group leaders would be encouraged to be examples in these areas and have conversations with group members to encourage them. They also encouraged their group leaders to facilitate an atmosphere of openness and confession in the groups.

When someone new moved in to place their membership with the church, a careful talk was held to make sure that the person understood "belonging" and being "devoted" and would commit to these principles. However, they did not feel they had biblical warrant to ask people to be in a specific one-on-one relationship. If this happened, it was good, but it was something they wanted to leave to individuals. All the leaders did agree that they would often share with the congregation from their own lives about their relationships.

TIME FOR EVALUATION

After a year each church reviewed how things had gone.

Sierra Vista

At Sierra Vista, some people had been thrilled to have a definite, clearly defined program. They enjoyed their relationships and felt they were once again getting needed discipling. Others had never been very satisfied with the people they were matched up with (though the leaders had invited people to talk with them about any arrangements that did not seem best). Some had struggled with leaders "imposing" these relationships. Some of those people had moved to a different congregation.

In some situations two weaker people had been matched, and neither showed the needed initiative. In those cases it seemed consistency of times together was quite poor.

Overall, however, the leaders of the church felt that the practice of this plan helped the church do much more effective shepherding, especially in marriage and dating issues. Some who had been hiding pornography habits got those out in the light and started to deal with them. Some with leadership potential got more attention.

During the year there were considerable problems as new people were added to the body. The leaders tried to be sure that no one had too much of a load to carry with the one-on-one commitments.

As the year ended, the leaders did feel a heavy burden for arranging pairings for a new year. It did not look like it would be any easier the second time around. Do you leave people together if it is working well? Do you mix it up? But when asked if they had second thoughts about their plan, they said, "No."

Saratoga

Saratoga reported that overall they were encouraged. Some of the groups did have a bit of trouble working out the pairings. In many cases most everyone in the group wanted to be partnered with the leader, but then saw that would be impossible. Several groups got back with the leaders suggesting a rotation that would have people changing partners every four to six months. That was approved, allowing the small group leaders to spend more time with several people and allowing the group members to get to know others much better. As new people were added, the groups figured out how to integrate them, and sometimes that meant some shifting around even before the four or six months was up.

As the new year approached, there was no church-wide need to work out a new schematic. Each group was handling the connections on its own. Overall, it seemed that the disciples at Saratoga felt they were respected and that their needs were met.

Northport

As Wayne Johnson and others at Northport continued to preach and teach on the "one another" theme, the level of openness and realness in their small groups did increase. There were outstanding examples in the church of people who connected with each other in purposeful and prayerful ways, but there were also people who flew below the radar and eventually developed problems that were pretty far along before anyone knew about them. If a problem did seem to be developing, there was a tendency for people to think "I'm not really the one to get with them" along with "I am sure someone else will." "Someone" seldom showed up.

In questioning the leaders of each church, it seemed the highest level of frustration and disappointment was at Northport. They wanted to see godly relationships, and were encouraged by reports from small groups. But they felt that too many issues of sin and conflict were not being addressed effectively, and they had work to do.

If you are a church leader, you and your fellow leaders will need to wrestle with issues that faced these churches. We will say it again: You will need to wrestle with these issues. *We are called to a "one another" life. Your church is called to a "one another" life.* How will you encourage it and nourish it? If you are not a church leader, appreciate the responsibility your leaders have. Talk with them, share your views, but in the end be ready to support them.

The kingdom is most certainly not shown to the world by some political maneuvering or grab for power. It is not even shown primarily through our long, personal times of prayer, our careful scholarship or our array of programs. It is shown supremely through the way we love—that is, "are committed to"—one another (John 13:34–35). However we decide to foster these relationships and create a culture where they will grow and abound, there should be no doubt in anyone's mind that we are going to live a "one-another life."

Wherever we have been, wherever our church is right now, let us begin. Let us begin today.

Making It Real

1. What plan have you already been working on to strengthen your own relationships?
2. What has been the most encouraging thing that has happened so far?
3. What can you do to encourage relationships in your congregation?
4. What conviction do you have about relationships that you want to hold on to for the rest of your life?

Appendix One
Philippians: A Study of Relationships

> Whatever happens, conduct yourselves in a manner worthy of the gospel of Christ. "live as citizens who reflect the Good News about Christ" (God's Word Translation); "live as citizens of heaven, conducting yourselves in a manner worthy of the Good News about Christ (New Living Translation). Then, whether I come and see you or only hear about you in my absence, I will know that you stand firm in one spirit, contending as one man for the faith of the gospel. (Philippians 1:27)

Some commentators see the letter to the Philippians as a collection of encouragements, exhortations and challenges without any central theme. One commentator says the theme is the generic "Living the Christian Life." We see it differently. We see Philippians teaching that "living as citizens of God's kingdom in a manner worthy of the gospel" is centrally about living as "partners in the gospel" (1:5), "abounding in love" (1:9), living "for your joy and progress in the faith" (i.e., living for others) (1:25), and being together in one spirit and being united as one man for the faith of the gospel (1:27). In other words, we see the theme as the relationships we have with one another.

The gospel is about a man laying down his life for others. A life worthy of (appropriate to) the gospel is a life where we lay down our lives for others. That theme runs all through Philippians. To live as a disciple is to be connected to others, to care for others, to give to others, to stay united with others.

What Paul says here at the end of chapter 1 sets things up for where he is going next in chapter 2—"tenderness and compassion," "being like-minded, having the same love, being one in spirit and purpose," and "consider others better than yourselves" (vv1-4). And then comes the great passage about the one man who laid down his life for others (vv5-11) and the call for us to have the same mind or attitude.

In verses 12 and 13 we have a passage often referred to:

> Therefore, my dear friends, as you have always obeyed—not only in my presence, but now much more in my absence—continue to work out your salvation with fear and trembling, for it is God who works in you to will and to act according to his good purpose. (Philippians 2:12-13)

Generally, we discuss this scripture out of the context in which it appears here. Having already noted what precedes it, it is good to look at what comes after it and then see the full context in which it is set.

In the last half of the chapter Paul presents three examples of Christians who are living for others:

a. Paul himself (v17)

> But even if I am being poured out like a drink offering on the sacrifice and service coming from your faith, I am glad and rejoice with all of you. So you too should be glad and rejoice with me.

b. Timothy (vv19-20)—"genuine interest in your welfare"

c. Epaphroditus (vv25, 30)—"my brother, fellow worker and fellow soldier...risking his life to make up for the help you could not give me."

The constant theme through chapter 1 and chapter 2 is partnership, fellowship, affection, unity, connection and laying down our lives for our brothers and sisters. He shares openly about how he feels about it, teaches about it, and gives examples to illustrate it.

That being true, how should we read verses 12 and 13?

In this context what has salvation brought us? Is it not a relationship with God and relationships with each other? Have we not been saved from the world of empty and broken relationships? We know that "working out our salvation" does not mean working for our salvation (3:9 in this letter, other places), so working it out must refer to expressing it, putting it to work, letting it do what it is meant to do. And so in this context it seems to us that working out your salvation has everything to do with working in your relationships and working for your relationships.

The call to do this with "fear and trembling" may seem to refer to something that is uniquely in our relationship with God and might cause some to think this is not referring to human relationships. But consider a most interesting fact. The only other times fear and trembling are referred to in the New Testament are both occasions when Paul is talking about human relationships:

- 1 Corinthians 2:3: "I came to you in weakness and fear, and with much trembling."
- 2 Corinthians 7:15: "And his [Timothy's] affection for you is all the greater when he remembers that you were all

obedient, receiving him with fear and trembling."

And then we hear in Philippians 2 (v13) "for it is God who works in you to will and to act according to his good purpose." Is God not at work in us all to bring us together? Is that not his very purpose (Ephesians 2:15)? Will not all the elements in the fruit of the Spirit, who is in us, cause us to show the greatest concern for one another?

In chapter 3, Paul is not dealing directly with relationships, but he is dealing with teaching (from "those dogs") that can disrupt the fellowship. In chapter 4 he is right back specifically to relationships:

> Therefore, my brothers, you whom I love and long for, my joy and crown, that is how you should stand firm in the Lord, dear friends! I plead with Euodia and I plead with Syntyche to agree with each other in the Lord. Yes, and I ask you, loyal yokefellow, help these women who have contended at my side in the cause of the gospel, along with Clement and the rest of my fellow workers, whose names are in the book of life. (Philippians 4:1–3)

He is back to personal expressions of affection—"my brothers, you whom I love and long for..." "dear friends!" (v1).

He specifically addresses by name two sisters whose relationship is in some way broken (v2). He calls on them to come back together in the Lord. We can only guess that these hardworking women who had contended for the gospel had considerable influence in the church and that their conflict would have affected others. It is an intriguing thing that Paul addresses them in a letter to be read publicly in the church.

He calls on a "yokefellow" (now there is a relationship term!)

to get with these two sisters and help them resolve their issue.

In teaching on Philippians 4:4–9 how many of us have been guilty of paying no attention to the context at all? As an advocate of "context, context, context," I (Tom) must plead guilty. I have failed in my own reading of this. But think with me now of the passage in the context of "right relationships as the manner worthy of the gospel."

> Rejoice in the Lord always. I will say it again: Rejoice! Let your gentleness be evident to all. The Lord is near. Do not be anxious about anything, but in everything, by prayer and petition, with thanksgiving, present your requests to God. And the peace of God, which transcends all understanding, will guard your hearts and your minds in Christ Jesus. Finally, brothers, whatever is true, whatever is noble, whatever is right, whatever is pure, whatever is lovely, whatever is admirable—if anything is excellent or praiseworthy—think about such things. Whatever you have learned or received or heard from me, or seen in me—put it into practice. And the God of peace will be with you. (Philippians 4:4–9)

"Rejoice in the Lord always." I have taught much on that, and preached it often to myself. But let us assume for a moment that Paul has not left his relationship theme at all. Let us assume that the Philippians are worried about these disciples who are not united. After all that was just referred to. Paul is reminding them to stay focused on the Lord and the joy in him. And then he says something I always had trouble figuring out in this passage: "Let your gentleness be evident to all." It just didn't seem to quite fit with rejoice and not be anxious. But when we think about a relationship context it makes much sense. Paul seems to be saying, "As you work through these relationship challenges, keep rejoicing in the Lord, and keep showing gentleness [patience or consideration] to one another, trusting that the Lord is near."

And then we could keep reading in this vein and hear: "Don't be anxious about these relationships, but pray about them and let God guard your heart and give you peace." Do the principles about rejoicing, praying and finding peace apply to many situations in our lives? Absolutely. But it may very well be that Paul first wrote these to dear friends whom he loved and longed for with the affection of Jesus, to help them in their relationships. Holding on to that idea, look at what comes next:

> Finally, brothers, whatever is true, whatever is noble, whatever is right, whatever is pure, whatever is lovely, whatever is admirable—if anything is excellent or praiseworthy—think about such things. Whatever you have learned or received or heard from me, or seen in me—put it into practice. And the God of peace will be with you. (Philippians 4:8-9)

Should we think that Paul spoke of this troubled relationship in the church and then randomly moved on to a general philosophy about thinking positively? We don't think so. When relationships are strained, what is the best thing to do? Isn't it to focus on what is right and admirable and praiseworthy in someone's life? In a marriage, in a strained friendship or in whatever relationship, is not that what helps people get their perspective? If both of these sisters had worked hard and contended for the gospel, would not they be well served by putting the emphasis on the right things in each other's lives?

Paul ends Philippians (vv10-23) first, by talking more about his relationship with the Philippian Christians (vv10-19), second, by praising God (v20) and finally, by speaking three times of Christians "greeting" each other (vv20-23). The word *aspazomai* means literally to "enfold in the arms," and is often translated "embrace." Paul began this letter talking about showing the affection of Jesus, and he ends it with the warmest kind of relationship terminology.

As we read it, to live "a life worthy of the gospel" means first and foremost being in relationships where we love, listen, are considerate, are humble and let others help us work out our differences, so we might "as one man contend together for the gospel."

Appendix Two
Discipling Relationships and the Holy Spirit

This article was written by James Gitre from Austin, Texas, and appeared on the Disciples Today Web site in March 2008. We thought that it was a good complement to the book and that it amplifies particularly the information in chapter 6. It is included here with the permission of the author and the DT Web site. Our thanks to both.

As the years have gone by as a Christian, I am amazed by the way that God works through discipling, or one-another, relationships. It's sometimes messy and not always pretty, but somehow God works. He works despite our weaknesses, sins and failures.[1]

Consequently, my faith is strengthened by the knowledge that I worship a God who can use less-than-perfect instruments to accomplish his perfect ends. Just what end does God seek in our discipling relationships? "Until Christ is formed in [us]" is the way Paul expressed it (Galatians 4:19).

This article, however, is not a defense for these types of relationships—others have already done this.[2] But we might ask ourselves: if discipling relationships have Christ-likeness, or transformation, as their goal, are we using all available means to

---

1. Some have hastily dismissed these relationships, citing shortcomings, but I think that gives man too much credit and God too little. The presence of failures does not prove the practice is inherently wrong. If this was true then we might we reconsider marriage or child-rearing since the same argument could be levied against them for all of us have made mistakes in these relationships.

2. For example, see *The Power of Discipling* by Gordon Ferguson (DPI) or *Master Plan of Discipleship* by Robert Coleman (Revell).

accomplish this task? Is it possible that in our efforts to practice what God has commanded, we have overlooked something? This is the question this article seeks to explore. With this in mind, consider the following:

> And we, who with unveiled faces all reflect the Lord's glory, are being transformed into his likeness with ever-increasing glory, which comes from the Lord, who is the Spirit. (2 Corinthians 3:18)
>
> I pray that out of his glorious riches he may strengthen you with power through his Spirit in your inner being, so that Christ may dwell in your hearts through faith. (Ephesians 3:16–17a)
>
> And if the Spirit of him who raised Jesus from the dead is living in you, he who raised Christ from the dead will also give life to your mortal bodies through his Spirit, who lives in you. Therefore, brothers, we have an obligation—but it is not to the sinful nature, to live according to it. For if you live according to the sinful nature, you will die; but if by the Spirit you put to death the misdeeds of the body, you will live, because those who are led by the Spirit of God are sons of God. (Romans 8:11–14)
>
> ...who have been chosen according to the foreknowledge of God the Father, through the sanctifying work of the Spirit, for obedience... (1 Peter 1:2)

In one way or another from different angles, each of the above passages touches upon the concept of transformation into Christ-likeness,[3] which, as we have stated, is the goal of discipling relationships. What you might not have noticed is that each of the above passages also speaks about the Spirit as primary to this work. That is, through the Spirit we participate in a transformational ministry that is even more glorious than the one given to Moses, glowing face and all (2 Corinthians 3:18); we have power in our inner being to realize Christ in us (Ephesians 3:16); we are given resurrection-life to defeat sin (Romans 8:13); and, finally, we are sanctified for obedience (1 Peter 1:2). All of this is accomplished by the ministry of the Holy Spirit. Consider the following observation by Sinclair Ferguson:

> The only resources for such sanctification are in Christ. Our sanctification is Christ's sanctification of himself in our humanity progressively applied to and realized in us through the ministry of the Holy Spirit.[4]

This author makes a crucial point: our transformation is not merely a human process, but a divine imperative wrought by the Holy Spirit. This is the same Spirit that brought us into union with Christ. And this is the same Spirit in every baptized disciple of Jesus.

So, then, we pause to consider the implications of the above upon our discussion: namely, if God intended for our discpling relationships to help form Christ in one another and God gave his Spirit for this same reason,[5] how do we interact with one another so that we work in harmony with God's Spirit, not apart from Him? This is a dimension that I believe we have yet to fully realize.

---

3. This can alternately be referred to as "sanctification," or some even use the term "Christoformity."

4. See *The Holy Spirit* by Sinclair Ferguson (Downer's Grove, IL: InterVarsity Press, 1997).

5. There are other dimensions to the presence of the Holy Spirit, but we explore this one for our purposes.

To answer this question and further our inquiry, we will briefly examine the relationship between the Spirit and the individual disciple where sin is concerned. Why focus on sin? Simply put, it is the mortal enemy that threatens our progress in discipleship, seeking to ensnare us at every opportunity and devour our spiritual vitality (Hebrews 12:1). In short, sin is at the front line of the spiritual battle. Therefore, if we can gain a more biblically informed perspective about the Spirit in this area, then, I believe, we will be better equipped to expand our theological horizons elsewhere. To that end, let's consider the following:

> Do you not know that he who unites himself with a prostitute is one with her in body? For it is said, "The two will become one flesh." But he who unites himself with the Lord is one with him in spirit.
> Flee from sexual immorality. All other sins a man commits are outside his body, but he who sins sexually sins against his own body. Do you not know that your body is a temple of the Holy Spirit, who is in you, whom you have received from God? You are not your own. (1 Corinthians 6:16–19)

In combating sexual immorality, Paul's words have direct bearing on our discussion. Following one of his many "don't you know" statements of the Corinthian correspondence (v19), Paul says something of great significance and import: we are a temple of God by his Spirit. Sins against the body have a dimension that goes beyond the physical act. It is sin against the very Spirit of God that dwells inside, and it is like joining the physical members of Christ in this sinful activity. This is a repulsive thought, and one that should sober us.[6]

---

6. We also see a similar warning furnished by the writer of Hebrews. To continue in willful and unrepentant sin is to trample upon the blood sacrifice of God's Son and to insult the Holy Spirit, giver of grace (see Hebrews 10:29).

Perhaps we might dismiss this warning if we have not engaged in sexual immorality. But all of us have enlisted the members of our body as mercenaries for sin in one way or another at one time or another, whether through lust of the eyes on the Internet, or the greed of feet in chasing after wealth, or countless other sins. Let's consider another passage along this same thread:

> Surely you heard of him and were taught in him in accordance with the truth that is in Jesus. You were taught, with regard to your former way of life, to put off your old self, which is being corrupted by its deceitful desires; to be made new in the attitude of your minds; and to put on the new self, created to be like God in true righteousness and holiness.... And do not grieve the Holy Spirit of God, with whom you were sealed for the day of redemption. (Ephesians 4:21–24, 30)

In the above, Paul admonishes the Ephesian disciples to "put off" the old self and "put on" the new self in response to "the truth that is in Jesus." After enumerating a number of specific sinful attitudes and behaviors to "put off," Paul concludes by explaining that to live in a way contrary to our high calling is to grieve the very Spirit of God. What can we learn from this? Namely, when you and I sin, our sin encounters God's Spirit. We do not sin alone. And we do not sin apart. The campaign of violence against our souls is not waged in darkness or in obscurity. It is witnessed by the Holy Spirit. And He is not neutral about sin.

Having examined the interplay between our sin and the response this provokes from the Spirit, we are now, I believe, ready to return to our main discussion and thus draw several conclusions that will allow us to advance our goal of working in harmony with the Spirit in our one-another relationships in a wholesome manner.

First, since God's Spirit is in each disciple, we should treat one another with respect. Don't read on too quickly. Let this set in. Often times in my zeal to deal with others' sin, I have not always acted in a way that properly recognizes and affirms that they, too, are sanctified by God's Spirit. Consider Paul's words to the church at Corinth, a church not widely recognized for its spiritual fidelity:

> To the church of God in Corinth, to those sanctified in Christ Jesus and called to be holy, together with all those everywhere who call on the name of our Lord Jesus Christ—their Lord and ours.... (1 Corinthians 1:2)

> But you were washed, you were sanctified, you were justified in the name of the Lord Jesus Christ and by the Spirit of our God. (1 Corinthians 6:11b)

Even while addressing some very disturbing issues—sexual immorality, incest, drunkenness, factions, just to name a few—Paul still recognizes these sin-laden Christians as vessels of God's Spirit.[7] He even went as far as to claim them as a letter of commendation from Christ, inked by this same Spirit:

> You yourselves are our letter, written on our hearts, known and read by everybody. You show that you are a letter from Christ, the result of our ministry, written not with ink but with the Spirit of the living God, not on tablets of stone but on tablets of human hearts.

---

7. This is not to suggest a tolerance for sin. Paul was on a rescue mission to restore a church that was desperately sick and in spiritual danger. His letter bears out several strong warnings. Yet, he purposely reminded them of where they had come from and whose they were.

> Such confidence as this is ours through Christ before God. (2 Corinthians 3:2–4)

So, too, we must strive to pierce the thick, suffocating shroud of sin to allow the fire of the Spirit to guide each other back to Jesus, back to the cross. With love we should inspire one another to live up to his or her privileged position in Christ as love-ransomed children of the King. Otherwise we run the risk of viewing each other as "problems to be solved" rather than "mysteries" to be enjoyed.[8] The former leads to looking down upon each other; the latter looks upwards towards Christ.

Second, let the Spirit do the convicting.

> When he comes, he will convict the world of guilt in regard to sin and righteousness and judgment. (John 16:8)

When it comes to confronting sin, realize that the Holy Spirit is also working to convict the individual. He or she might have ignored it or constructed rationalizations to support his/her actions, but the Spirit doesn't let sin slide. For our part, we can assist in this process by bringing the word of God, the sword of the Spirit (Ephesians 6:17), to bear upon the situation.

> For the word of God is living and active. Sharper than any double-edged sword, it penetrates even to dividing soul and spirit, joints and marrow; it judges the thoughts and attitudes of the heart. (Hebrews 4:12)

All of us who became Christians can testify how powerfully God's Spirit worked to bring us to repentance from a life of sin and godlessness. Do we think this divine activity stops once we get on the other side of the cross?

---

8. Luke Timothy Johnson, *Living Jesus* (San Francisco: Harper Collins, 1998), 58.

So when we need to have one of those difficult talks, we can have confidence that God's Spirit is working in concert with us to bring the individual back towards repentance and into a reconciled relationship with God.

Third, we can leave room for the Spirit to work. When we have talked with a brother or sister and have been frank and honest with our concerns, and this has not met with an appropriate response at first, we can continue to take up the matter with confidence to know that God, too, is working through his Spirit.[9] The Holy Spirit is not passive. He is working. It might not come to the kind of dramatic and decisive conclusion as seen in Acts chapter five with Ananias and Sapphira, but it does not go unnoticed. God will reveal men's sins. Consequently, sometimes we need to give God space to work. There are no "free" sins.

With the above points in mind, how then can we bring the Spirit to bear upon our relationships? Simply put, we can include the Spirit in our discussions with one another. As an example, in a recent conversation I had with a brother where a particular sin continued to manifest itself despite numerous previous attempts to address it, I asked the brother: "How do you suppose the Holy Spirit feels about this?" He correctly responded that his actions (or lack thereof) were grieving the Holy Spirit.

This line of questioning threw the discussion along a whole new axis and put matters in an entirely different frame of reference. No more prodding or persuading on my part was needed. It was now his decision whether to continue along the same course of action or to turn towards God in repentance.

---

9. This statement does not take into account incidents that require formal church discipline.

This is no clever ministry parlor trick; it is in keeping with the numerous passages that point us towards the Spirit as the core of the Christian life. Indeed, we cannot even live the life apart from the power of the Spirit. Witness Paul's careful exhortation below:

> For God did not call us to be impure, but to live a holy life. Therefore, he who rejects this instruction does not reject man but God, who gives you his Holy Spirit. (1 Thessalonians 4:7–8)

Paul could have ended his appeal by saying that they were rejecting God (and this would have been sufficient!). But Paul, guided by the Holy Spirit, reminded them that the presence of the Spirit was a gift from God. Rejection of the call to holiness was not a rejection of man. It was a rejection of God, who gave the Spirit. In doing this, Paul kept the Spirit in view to stimulate their thinking towards holy living. So, too, we should remind one another that we bear a divine gift (and it is a gift). We are made holy by God's Spirit, and we continue in holiness by this same Spirit.

In conclusion, I believe that if we are to be more effective in our interactions with one another, we must give due consideration to the belief that the Spirit is actively working inside each disciple. Furthermore, we need to respond in such a way so that we work in harmony with the Spirit to continuously reconcile each other to God in ever-increasing faithfulness (2 Corinthians 5:18). I believe it is a dimension that is worth our careful consideration and prayerful exploration.

Under His Mercy,
James Gitre